BIRDING
AUSTRALIA'S
ISLANDS

BIRDING AUSTRALIA'S ISLANDS

Sue Taylor

JOHN BEAUFOY PUBLISHING

First published in the United Kingdom and Australia in 2019 by John Beaufoy Publishing,
11 Blenheim Court, 316 Woodstock Road, Oxford OX2 7NS, England
www.johnbeaufoy.com

10 9 8 7 6 5 4 3 2 1

ISBN 978-1-912081-13-4

Edited by Krystyna Mayer
Designed by Gulmohur
Project management by Rosemary Wilkinson

Printed and bound in Malaysia by Times Offset (M) Sdn. Bhd.

Title pages: The Lacepedes are important for breeding Lesser Frigatebirds.

Contents

Introduction

This is my story of birding on some of Australia's very special islands. Of course, I don't attempt to include every Australian island – there are, so they tell me, 8,371 of them. How did I select the islands to be included in this book? They're not the biggest or even necessarily the best birding islands. Quite inadvertently, I've managed to include Australia's most extreme islands: the most southerly (Macquarie Island), most northerly (Boigu Island, which just pips Christmas Island by one degree), most westerly (Cocos Islands) and most easterly (Norfolk Island). It was not my intention to go to extremes. My aim was very simple: to include islands where I've had fun birding. I may have seen lots of birds there. I may have seen several lifers, or even several birds never seen before in Australia. Or I may have enjoyed special encounters with common birds.

Who hasn't dreamt of escaping to an island? There's something very romantic about being cut off from the tumult of twenty-first century civilization and feeling totally isolated, all alone with nature. Whether it's due to seeing fluttering coconut palms and ethereal White Terns on the Cocos Islands, or lumbering elephant seals among a mind-boggling 100,000 King Penguins on Macquarie Island, it's certainly an unforgettable experience. The birder is positively privileged to be present.

Birders wanting to see every Australian bird must visit Lord Howe, Norfolk, Christmas and Macquarie Islands. Serious twitchers looking for rare vagrants visit Ashmore Reef and the Torres Strait. All Tasmania's endemics can be seen on Bruny Island. Common Pheasants, Wild Turkeys and Indian Peafowl can be seen on King Island in Bass Strait. King Quail are reputedly resident on French Island in Western Port Bay – I didn't see any on either of my visits.

I've visited most of the featured islands just once, although I've returned to a couple of places when I failed to see my target species on the first occasion. I've visited Christmas Island four times and have booked to go back for my fifth visit this year. However, that's not because I've dipped on the endemics, but because it's such a special place and the birds just keep getting better and better. Not only are there more birders going to more exciting places today, but there are also more vagrants being blown in from exotic shores. Moreover, with today's instant communication, everyone knows that a Corn Crake has been seen on an old Christmas Island mine site within hours of its discovery.

The islands in this book are accessed by various methods, mostly by boat, some by plane, some by ferry, one by bridge and one by water taxi. Some are not accessed at all. I haven't actually set foot on three of the featured islands: two are nature reserves and not accessible to the public – that's Cabbage Tree Island off Port Stephens in New South Wales and Raine Island in far north Queensland. The third is Browse Island in far north Western Australia, where the seas were too rough for me to disembark.

In 1989 I set out to see as many Australian birds as possible. At first my goal was 600 species. Then it became 700. Then 800. Now I know 900 is out of the question, but could I possibly get to 850 one day? It took me until 2017 to reach the magic milestone of 800. I couldn't have done it without visiting Australia's unique islands. Needless to say, I have not seen every Australian bird. I don't suppose I ever will – but it is great fun trying.

Now, just a quick word about names and taxonomy. Research into our avifauna is ongoing. Species are forever being split and lumped, and decisions are always controversial. When international authorities decide that Intermediate Egrets seen on Christmas Island are a different species from the Plumed Egrets seen on the Australian mainland, birders want to count both species, naturally – and they want to do it now, not in a decade's time when the official list is reissued.

Australian birders used to rely on a list compiled by Les Christidis and Walter E. Boles, which was first published in 1994. At that time, Les Christidis was Curator of Birds at the Museum of Victoria in Melbourne, and Walter Boles was Scientific Officer in the Ornithology Section and Collection Manager of Terrestrial Vertebrates at the Australian Museum in Sydney. Their list was updated in 2008. Soon after this, Christidis and Boles let it be known that they did not intend to undertake any further updates of the list, and birders immediately looked for an alternative reliable authority with regular updates. Most Australian birders now use the International Ornithological Congress (IOC) list, which is updated twice annually. You can find the list at www.worldbirdnames.org. If you go to Tony Palliser's Birders Totals page (www.tonypalliser.com), you will find a link to the Australian IOC list. I'm presently using IOC version 8.2, which is the most up-to-date version at the time of writing.

There are other lists with their own loyal adherents, and just to provide confusion, BirdLife Australia maintains its own list. Thus while some birders talk about the White-headed Stilt, others call the same bird Black-winged Stilt or even Pied Stilt. Ne'er the twain shall meet.

My advice is to avoid these unnecessary controversies and enjoy watching Australia's beautiful birds, and to go to the wonderful islands and experience their very special birds. I'm sure you'll have as much fun as I've had – and am still having.

1 Macquarie Island

I expected a great deal from my trip to Macquarie Island. I expected to be terrified and delighted. I imagined I'd be apprehensive and exhilarated. I feared I'd be humiliated and embarrassed. As it happened, I was never terrified. Of course what I really wanted out of the trip was to add ten birds to my lifelist.

KEY SPECIES
King Penguin
Gentoo Penguin
Chinstrap Penguin
Southern Rockhopper
Royal Penguin
Black-bellied Storm Petrel
Grey-headed Albatross
Soft-plumaged Petrel
Macquarie Shag
Antarctic Tern
Lesser Redpoll

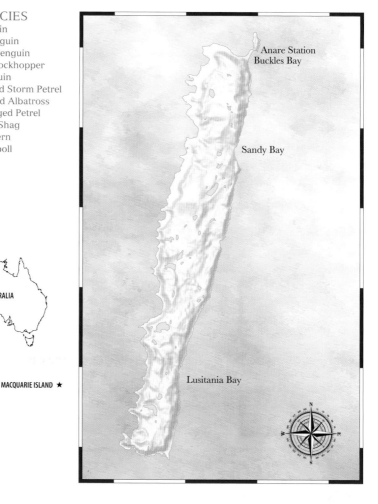

AUSTRALIA

MACQUARIE ISLAND ★

Right: Buckles Bay, Macquarie Island.

Everyone I knew who'd been to Macquarie Island spoke about the experience with inspired reverence. Without exception, their eyes lit up as if they'd witnessed the second coming. They erupted with contagious enthusiasm. They were unanimous: Macquarie Island was the trip of a lifetime.

I travelled with Heritage Expeditions on *The Spirit of Enderby* in December 2009, with 43 other intrepid tourists. There were also 13 staff and 22 Russian crew on this 72m research vessel. Our leader, Nathan, despite appearing to be disconcertingly young, proved to be a wonderful leader. We left from the Port of Bluff, near Invercargill on the South Island of New Zealand. Other tour companies also visit the subantarctic. On Macquarie, they told me that nine cruise ships visit each season (that's between December and February), so there must be plenty of choice. If you chose to go with another company you may have superior guides and accommodation, but you could not possibly enjoy superior food. Our meals were unsurpassed.

This was my first (and only) trip to New Zealand. I was most impressed as I flew over the spectacular Southern Alps; I was fascinated with Invercargill Museum's tuatara breeding programme, and extremely envious of the government's attitude to pest eradication. But the problem for me in leaving from a foreign port was that most of the time I was in foreign waters and the birds I saw did not count for my Australian list.

It was a 12-day trip: it took five days to get to Macquarie – it is, after all, halfway to the Antarctic. I spent most of the time on the bridge. The seas were extremely rough and on some days we were advised not to leave our bunks. Luckily, when this happened in Australian waters I was already on the bridge. This did not prevent me from being tossed around like an ice cube in a cocktail shaker, but it did stop me from being thrown into the Southern Ocean. It also gave me good views of passing seabirds in an acceptable ambient temperature. The alternative was to go on deck, which was not only freezing cold but slippery and dangerous. My routine was simple and it worked. I followed it on my subsequent trip to the Antarctic and it worked then too. Half an hour before I got up I swallowed a Travacalm, ate a dry biscuit and lay flat for 30 minutes. I was never seasick when I followed this routine.

We'd left Bluff at 3 p.m. on Friday, 18 December 2009, and visited The Snares, Auckland Island and Enderby Island. We reached Australian waters on the following Tuesday. At last, the birds I saw could be counted on my Australian list.

The first species I saw were Black-bellied Storm Petrels. Ironically, Black-bellied and White-bellied Storm Petrels are very difficult to tell apart, as both can have

The first birds I saw in Australian waters were Black-bellied Storm Petrels.

Then I saw a Grey-headed Albatross.

varying amounts of black on their bellies. But White-bellied birds are more tropical in distribution. One handy distinguishing feature is that the feet of Black-bellied birds extend beyond the tail in flight. A small flock flew close to the boat and I could see the protruding feet of the birds. This was my first tickable species for the trip, and I felt good.

Then I saw a Grey-headed Albatross, a bird I'd longed to see for many years. At that time I was using Christidis and Boles 2008 taxonomy, and (apart from the vagrant northern hemisphere Laysan Albatross sighted once on Norfolk Island that I never expect to see), this was my last Australian albatross species. It's a good feeling to finalize a family. Today, using IOC taxonomy, I am missing another two species

(Tristan and Chatham Albatrosses). Christidis and Boles recognized 10 Australian albatrosses (including the vagrant Laysan), whereas IOC presently lists 17.

I was feeling pretty pleased with myself. The Grey-headed Albatross was my 698th Australian bird. We'd arrive at Macquarie Island the next day, and I felt sure I'd achieve what was at that time my milestone target of 700 Australian birds (if you'd told me less than a decade ago that by now I would have seen more than 800 Australian birds, I'd have been quite incredulous).

I didn't like leaving the bridge while we were in Australian waters, and I didn't like attending films or lectures in the horrible lecture theatre downstairs. Here the seats were not fixed to the floor, and they moved with the swell of the sea. When one went over it had a domino effect, and rows of seats (and their occupants) crashed to the floor. Notwithstanding these dangerous conditions, I felt obliged to attend the introductory lecture about Macquarie Island, given by the nature guide. Let's call him Brian, though that's not his real name.

Brian told us that Macquarie Island was located 1,200km south of New Zealand, 1,500km south-south-east of Tasmania, right on the Antarctic Convergence. It is 34km long and up to 5km wide. The island has a narrow continental shelf, which matters because that's where breeding seabirds forage. It has 41 native plant species, but there are no woody plants. It was declared a wildlife sanctuary in 1933 and listed as a World Heritage Area in 1997. Today it is administered by the Tasmanian Parks and Wildlife Service and accommodates a permanent base of the Australian National Antarctic Research Expeditions (ANARE). The weather station on Macquarie has been keeping records since 1948 and hence provides useful data to enable scientists to assess the rate of global warming. I was stifling a yawn. Brian droned on.

While most subantarctic islands originated from underwater volcanoes (said Brian) Macquarie was squeezed up from 6km beneath the ocean floor. It is the only place in the world where geologists can study the exposed oceanic crust. The sand is black because it is derived from dark basaltic rocks. Geologically speaking, Macquarie Island is very young – the oldest rocks are just 11.5 million years old. Macquarie is still seismically active and every year there is an earthquake measuring 6.2 on the Richter scale; every decade there is an earthquake measuring 7.2.

Brian went on to say that Macquarie Island is home to many interesting birds. Now he was broaching a subject I cared about. I sat up and listened. The island supports 3.5 million breeding seabirds. That's quite a number. The most obvious birds are the penguins. There are 800,000 breeding pairs of Royal Penguins (native to Macquarie Island); 300,000–400,000 Southern Rockhopper Penguins (Macquarie's

There are 800,000 breeding pairs of Royal Penguins on Macquarie Island.

There are 4,000–5,000 breeding pairs of Gentoo Penguins on the island.

smallest penguin); about 100,000 King Penguins (which apparently have the longest breeding cycle of any bird – I made a note to check that later); and 4,000–5,000 breeding pairs of Gentoo Penguins. There are four species of albatross – Black-browed, Grey-headed, Light-mantled and Wandering. There are both Northern and Southern Giant Petrels, including the white morph of the latter. The Macquarie Shag is most closely related to the Blue-eyed Shag of North America. There are about 30 breeding pairs of Antarctic Terns on Macquarie. I grinned inanely. Here were six species I was hoping to tick – four penguins, the shag and the tern. I'd certainly reach 700 tomorrow.

Black-browed Albatross.

Light-mantled Albatross.

Wandering Albatross.

Later, back home in Melbourne, I researched the breeding cycle of King Penguins. Surely the Emperor, the largest penguin, standing over 1m tall, would have a longer breeding cycle than the smaller King? I learnt that incubation for the Emperor takes 60–65 days and for the King it is 54 days. Simplistically, it seemed that the assertion that Kings have the longest breeding cycle of any bird was wrong. I read further. The Emperor breeds from March to December. Its eggs are laid in May or June, and the chicks hatch in July or August and are brooded for 40 days. The parents feed the chicks until they depart in December. The King, on the other hand, lays eggs at anytime between November and March, broods the chick for 30 days, but feeds it

King Penguins have the longest breeding cycle of any bird.

for an incredible 10–30 months after hatching. So Brian was quite correct – the King Penguin has the longest breeding cycle of any bird. However, while the breeding cycle can last 14–16 months, parents seem to become more efficient over time and it is possible for King Penguins to raise two chicks in three years. Compare this with the Light-mantled Albatross, which can wait four years between breeding attempts, and you can understand the difference between having the longest breeding cycle and being the slowest breeder.

Brian also mentioned seals. There are three species of fur seal (and some interbreeding) – Antarctic, Subantarctic and New Zealand. The most numerous seal is the elephant seal (the males are four and a half times larger than the hapless females). The population had recovered from nineteenth-century sealing, but is now declining again. Scientists are trying to discover why. Leopard Seals are seen in winter and spring, and Hooker's Sea Lions visit regularly but do not breed on Macquarie.

The next subject covered by Brian was the pest-eradication programme, which at that time was still underway. It was declared a success in 2014, but when I was on the island in 2009 cats and Wekas had been eradicated, and the rabbits and rodents were about to be tackled. At that time the eradication programme was estimated to cost A\$24.6 million.

Brian then moved on to the weather. We were told that it rained nearly every day on Macquarie. It was also very windy and almost always misty. In mid-summer there are 18 hours of daylight each day, but you're lucky to get four hours of sunshine. The mean annual temperature is 4.4° C. At the time of my visit 15 people over-wintered on Macquarie each year, and about 30 were present in summer. Subsequently, there was talk of closing the ANARE base, but there was such a community backlash that politicians changed their minds and looked for cost savings elsewhere.

I'll never forget Wednesday, 23 December 2009. It was my brother's birthday and it was the day I saw my 700th Australian bird. It had been a bumpy night. Probably a better description is a slide-y night. Throughout the night, with a boring, mindless repetition, my mattress slid up and down in my bunk. There was hardly any room to spare – the mattress fitted the bunk snugly. Yet it managed to slide down, pause, then slide back. Then again. And again. Relentlessly, all night long. Breakfast was scheduled for 8.30 a.m., so I arose at 6.30 a.m. When it was rough it could take me an hour and a half to get dressed. I went straight to the bridge.

The day's programme was given with dual times. *Enderby* did not change its clocks, but as we were in Australian waters, Australian (eastern summer) time was given in brackets beside New Zealand time (that is to say, two hours earlier). Instead of our morning wake-up call, Nathan announced that it was too rough to serve breakfast, so the meal was postponed and we should all stay in bed. I was very pleased that I was already on the bridge. I hung on to the rail with both hands and watched Macquarie Island emerge from the mist. Word on the bridge was that we'd passed an iceberg during the night but that Nathan had judged that it was too rough to wake people up to see it.

I was delighted to see a Soft-plumaged Petrel fly past (no. 699). There are two phases of the Soft-plumaged Petrel. The light one (which I saw) and the dark one (which is rare). The light phase has dark underwings, a white belly with a grey breastband and a dark 'M' pattern on the upperwing. The dark phase is, well, darker. I was tickled pink to add the Soft-plumaged Petrel to my life list. This was a bird that I'd just missed out on seeing once before and the omission still rankled. I believe I was the only person on the boat to miss out. It was on a pelagic out of Eaglehawk Neck in Tasmania. Roger (my husband) and I had flown to Hobart, picked up our hire car and given a lift from the airport to Eaglehawk Neck to Jenny, a keen birder from country New South Wales who we'd met birding on Cocos Island.

I was delighted to see a Soft-plumaged Petrel.

The weather was rough on that particular day, as it can be out of Eaglehawk Neck. The waves were up to 5m high. Jenny became ill, but it was no simple seasickness. She was vomiting blood. A doctor on board proclaimed that if she had a ruptured oesophagus and vomited again she could die. This was pretty dramatic stuff. The captain turned to the nearest port and rang for an ambulance. It was so rough that we were instructed to keep the boat evenly balanced, that is to say, we should maintain the same number of birders on the port side as on the starboard side. Jenny was on her back in the cabin. Then the cry went up: 'Soft-plumaged Petrel!' Everyone rushed to the port side of the boat. The captain ordered people to keep the boat balanced. Obediently, alone, I stood miserably at starboard and missed out on seeing the Soft-plumaged Petrel. Jenny was taken to hospital and the boat trip was aborted. Back home in Melbourne a few days later, I phoned to see how she was. She was fine, she told me. What's more, she'd had unimpeded views of the Soft-plumaged Petrel from her sick bed.

It's this sort of thing that persuades the enthusiastic twitcher that there's no justice in the world. However, on 23 December 2009, as I'd just recorded my 699th Australian bird, I was not thinking about injustices. I was confidently, perhaps smugly, waiting for the next big tick. What would it be?

I was not left guessing for long, for very soon after I'd ticked the Soft-plumaged Petrel, a flotilla of Southern Rockhopper Penguins porpoised in front of the boat (no. 700). I'd achieved my target before breakfast – and what a great bird for the milestone. I'd secretly dreaded the possibility of ticking a redpoll at number 700 – I'd have been dismayed to have an exotic European interloper forever occupying that hallowed spot. I was chuffed to have the sweet little penguin as my 700th bird. It is the smallest of all the crested penguins, which can be difficult to tell apart, but the straw-coloured plumes on the Rockhopper don't reach its bill or meet across its forehead.

The daily programme that had shown us breakfasting at 8.30 a.m. also stated that we'd arrive at Buckles Bay at that time, and that at 9 a.m. we'd pick up some rangers from the Tasmanian Parks and Wildlife Service. In fact it was a little after 8.30 a.m. when we arrived at Buckles Bay, and it was far too rough to consider lowering Zodiacs, so we changed to plan B and cruised down the east coast of Macquarie Island to Lusitania Bay.

We could see Royal Penguins (no. 701) and King Penguins (no. 702) both on the shore and in the water around us, and elephant seals on the beach. I was pleased to see Macquarie Shags fly past (no. 703). Christidis and Boles called these Imperial

Royal and King Penguins parading past a sleeping seal.

Shags, and that's fine by me. Any name will do, as long as I can count them. Needless to say, I was pretty happy standing on the bridge, having seen 703 birds. What did I care if the rangers couldn't come on board? Who needed rangers? I was doing very nicely, thank you, without rangers.

Watching the penguins porpoising through the waves, I saw what was indisputably a Chinstrap Penguin (no. 704). The various crested penguins can be difficult to identify as they swim past in turbulent seas, but the distinct facial pattern of the Chinstrap Penguin cannot be confused with anything else. This bird had been on my secret wish list, but I hadn't dared to speak it out loud.

Another bird on my secret wish list was the Southern Fulmar. It is like a large gull with a pink bill. Once when I was alone on the bridge I did see a large white bird, flying very high. Its silhouette was like that of a feral pigeon. It was slate-grey above and pearly silvery-white below. I didn't see its bill colour. In frustration I looked around trying to find a witness to my sighting, preferably one with excellent eyesight and a camera. No one was there. Some years later I went to the Antarctic and saw many Southern Fulmars. They did not have the silhouette of a feral pigeon – they have elegant long wings. We will never know the identity of my mystery large white bird.

A Southern Fulmar, which I saw in the Antarctic, not on Macquarie.

When the weather improved we returned to Buckles Bay and picked up three rangers. Then there was another compulsory briefing in the treacherous lecture theatre. Nathan, our leader, spoke and repeated all the wildlife guidelines and conservation regulations we'd heard before. Give way to wildlife, avoid penguin walkways, stay at least 5m from all wildlife, move slowly, crouch down to penguin level to be less intimidating, don't touch the wildlife, don't surround the wildlife, don't disturb anything, obey instructions from rangers, don't stray from the beach. Then Nathan asked the head ranger politely if there was anything he'd like to add. I wish Nathan had asked if there was anything *new* he'd like to add, because the head ranger simply repeated, in an irritatingly soft voice, everything that Nathan had already told us.

At Sandy Bay we all lined up to get on to the Zodiacs, wearing our wet-weather gear and disinfected boots. There was no way of manipulating where you stood in the queue to select which (or, more importantly, whose) Zodiac you were on. It was always pot luck. I always wanted Nathan – and always ended up with Brian.

I have never mastered the art of getting on and off small boats. The knowledge that I was going to have to face up to this dominated my thinking throughout the trip. For people with short legs or poor balance or both, it can be a challenge stepping from a little boat into surging surf full of moving kelp concealing sharp rocks. It seems odd to me that no one else on the boat articulated the same anxiety that overwhelmed me throughout the trip. Gingerly I walked down the gangplank, keeping my trepidation to myself. At the bottom step a burly Russian crewman grabbed my left arm, Brian grabbed my right arm and I stepped on to the edge of the Zodiac as we'd been instructed. Then they let go, my wet boot slipped on the rubber rim of the Zodiac and I promptly fell on to my bottom on the floor of the boat.

'Oh!' I said, and felt 50 pairs of eyes on me.

'Get up!' yelled Brian. There was no mistaking the fury in his voice. Did he imagine I'd fallen deliberately? Or was he aware that he'd let go of me too soon?

Somehow, with assistance, I scrambled up to sit on the edge of the Zodiac. David, a big, quiet man from New York, helped me on my left.

'Are you all right?' he asked kindly. It was the first time he'd ever spoken to me.

'Yes, I'm fine, thanks,' I lied. I wasn't hurt, but I was humiliated. There was another, younger American on my right. He held out his arm.

'Hang on,' he offered with a grin. With a pathetic smile I accepted his offer. It was the first time I'd spoken to him too. I held his arm all the way to shore as the Zodiac bumped across the waves. I couldn't get off that boat quickly enough.

Here I was, actually on Macquarie Island, with a colony of Royal Penguins on my left and a colony of King Penguins on my right. I'd achieved my lifetime ambition of seeing 700 Australian birds, a quest that had taken me 20 years, and my mind was preoccupied with Brian's furious instruction. 'Get up!' I heard him yelling at me over and over again.

It couldn't last, of course. I agreed with Sir Douglas Mawson that 'This little island is one of the wonder spots of the world.' I was completely captivated by the penguins. They are so cute in their little dinner suits that it is almost impossible not to anthropomorphize. I tried hard to avoid their walkways as instructed but it wasn't always easy. When I found myself on a penguin pathway, I hurried out of the way.

Dave, a friendly New Zealand farmer who often helped me across the bridge when the seas were rough, reminded me to walk slowly near the penguins. He got down to penguin level. I took a wonderful series of photos of a Royal Penguin investigating Dave's camera, before Dave was aware of it. Then Nathan hailed me to say that there was a Gentoo Penguin in the water. I wandered along the beach, confident that the

'One of the wonder spots of the world.'

Gentoo had gone and that everyone else would have seen it, but I, the person who cared most, would miss out. I told myself to buck up. This was supposed to be the trip of a lifetime. I had everything to celebrate. And, as if on cue, there, swimming in the sea, was one single Gentoo Penguin (no. 705).

I turned back towards the Royal Penguins. The Kings are big and very photogenic with that colourful orange comma on their necks, but I loved the little Royals. These used to be considered Macaronis until someone noticed that on Macquarie Island they had white chins, while elsewhere they had black chins. Thus the Royals gained species status (except on the conservative official Australian list – Christidis and Boles – which at that time still regarded them as a race). These penguins did *not* all have white chins – some were white, some were pale grey and some were dark charcoal. Young birds have grey smudges around their faces. Now ornithologists believe that the birds on Macquarie are Royals and any Macaroni present is a vagrant.

At that time, December 2009, rabbits were obviously present in big numbers and I couldn't wait for the eradication programme to begin. I saw a skua swoop at a young bunny. The rabbit just managed to slip into a burrow in time to avoid being lunch. At the back of the beach two large elephant seals were fighting. I couldn't tell how serious it was – were they just posturing or did they mean it?

Two large elephant seals were fighting.

I took the first Zodiac back, and it was skippered by Nathan. I was back on board the *Enderby* at a quarter to six. I wanted a celebratory alcoholic drink but I was aware that dinner was a long way off, so I settled for coffee instead, chatting with other passengers. We all agreed that it had been a great day. We waited for tea – and waited. The last Zodiac was scheduled to return at 8.30 p.m., so dinner would not be before 9 p.m. If I hadn't arranged for everyone to have champagne to celebrate my 700 milestone, I'd have gone to bed. Nine o'clock was way too late for me. Finally, dinner was announced and I made my way downstairs to the dining room. I think everyone enjoyed the champagne, but I'm not sure that everyone understood what it was all about.

At six o'clock on Thursday morning I positively sprang out of my bunk, delighted with the calm conditions. We'd spent the night at anchor off Sandy Bay. I washed my hair quickly and hurried down to the deck. Here I watched a pair of Light-mantled Albatrosses doing their spectacular synchronized mating flight: a beautiful ballet that would inspire any choreographer. Then I saw Antarctic Terns (no. 706) and knew it was going to be a special day. I'd seen these terns before several times on this trip, but these were *Australian* Antarctic Terns. Their pristine white backs glistened, and I beamed happily.

When I saw an Antarctic Tern I knew it was going to be a special day.

While we had breakfast, the *Enderby* cruised back to Buckles Bay, site of the ANARE base with its famous meteorological dome. After breakfast I put on my wet gear and safety harness, grabbed my camera, disinfected my sea boots and waited in line for a Zodiac to take me ashore. The *Enderby* was now anchored in Buckles Bay. On the other side of the isthmus we could clearly see one huge blue iceberg. It was pretty impressive.

My Australian life total of 706 was good – but 707 would be better. There was still one bird missing from my Macquarie Island list: the Lesser Redpoll, the exotic little bird I'd been worried might insinuate itself into the landmark 700 position. Now that danger was past, I was very keen to get the bird on to my Australian list, and at that time this was the only place in the world where that was possible. Since then, some redpolls have been sighted on Lord Howe Island. But in 2009, I believed this was my one chance in a lifetime to add the redpoll to my Australian list. In times gone by it was thought that these birds were Common Redpolls, but ornithologists now believe that those on Macquarie Island are probably Lesser Redpolls and most likely hybrids at that.

Redpolls are European birds, introduced to New Zealand by homesick nineteenth-century Britons. The birds are sweet little things, smaller than a sparrow. Yet they managed to get to Macquarie Island from New Zealand by themselves – a trip of

The ANARE base with its famous meteorological dome.

Spirit of Enderby *in Buckles Bay.*

some 1,200km. Not a bad effort for such a small bird, you might think. But consider that at home in Europe they may spend summer in Iceland or northern Scandinavia, and winter in the south of France – a journey twice as long as that from New Zealand to Macquarie Island – and they do it every year, and back again.

My mind was occupied exclusively by redpolls as I walked down the gangplank to my Zodiac and realized that once again I was to be driven by Brian. I didn't fall over getting into the Zodiac: my second achievement for the day. And I managed to get off without drawing undue attention to myself. Things were going well.

We were to have a guided tour of the ANARE base. On the beach we were split into four groups. I learnt later that the four tours were as different as pelicans and pardalotes. Evidently there were no guidelines about what should or should not be included in the tour – guides could include whatever they liked. One group concentrated on the history of the base, and everyone who'd been on that tour enjoyed it particularly. Helen was my guide. Our tour didn't have a theme, although Helen's brother's attitude to her presence on Macquarie seemed to be cropping up constantly. She laughed when I asked (very politely) where to look for a redpoll.

'You're an Australian birder!' she accused me.

Once, when I wandered into the tussock following an insect-like *zzzt* call, Helen instructed me to stay on the gravel. Later I learnt that the endemic cushion plants are diseased, and this is no doubt a good reason for not walking on them and potentially spreading the affliction. I'd have been much happier obeying Helen's instruction if she'd told me this at the time. However, I suspect that diseased cushion plants were not foremost in her mind, because a little later one of the trip's official photographers (there were two) informed Helen that he must take a photograph. He disappeared out of sight with her blessing, trampling cushion plants with gay abandon.

On the beach we were surrounded by wildlife, mainly penguins and seals. There were Royal, King and Gentoo Penguins. There were lots of irresistibly cute weaner elephant seals. It was hard to believe that the young males would grow up to be as ugly as their fathers. There were big, lazy moulting males – I was pleased that none of yesterday's testosterone was in evidence today.

There were also skuas, Kelp Gulls, and both Northern and Southern Giant-Petrels, including several of the white morph of the latter. Occasionally I'd catch my breath when I first glimpsed one of these huge white birds, thinking momentarily it might be a fulmar. The white morph of the Southern Giant-Petrel is easily identified once you have a good look. It is not pure white at all – it has a few brown feathers scattered randomly throughout its plumage. I'd never seen the white morph before. It made it

We were surrounded by wildlife.

There were lots of irresistibly cute weaner elephant seals.

Northern Giant Petrel.

Southern Giant Petrel.

The white morph of the Southern Giant Petrel is called the White Nelly.

easy to know which giant-petrel it was, as only the Southern has the white morph. At sea I'm used to looking for the colour of the bill-tip to identify Southern from Northern birds: the Southern has a greenish bill-tip; the Northern has a reddish-brown one. At sea from a heaving boat it is not always easy to see the colour of the bill-tip of a bird flying past at a distance. Other people manage it, but I always struggle.

It's not surprising, really, that it took until the 1960s for ornithologists to decide that there were two species of giant petrel. 'Southern' and 'Northern' could be considered misleading names as both species occupy the same latitudes. Interestingly, the females take prey from the sea, while the slightly larger males scavenge on land from carcasses of penguins and seals.

As well as all these seabirds, there was a colony of Macquarie Shags on the rocks. As a backdrop to it all, there was that magic translucent blue iceberg.

Helen led us along the beach past the penguins and towards the mess. Everyone was busy preparing for Christmas celebrations. Our passports had been taken ashore to be imprinted with the Macquarie Island stamp. Here we could buy a postcard, and send it – as long as we didn't require prompt delivery. It would probably leave with the summer staff, when the winter team arrived in about five months' time. Helen seemed relieved to be rid of us. She didn't take us into the mess, but left us on the verandah with instructions to remove our boots before we went inside. I wasn't interested in visiting the mess. I didn't need nourishment: I required a redpoll. Why couldn't I go birding? Grudgingly, I did as I'd been told. I leant against the wall and

Some people just came to see an iceberg.

removed my boots, then managed to walk over the sharp iron grids in my socks without squealing too loudly. No one complained, but I did think it was not a very hospitable way to treat visitors. We had, after all, paid a fee for the privilege of visiting the island – and not seeing redpolls, I said to myself grumpily.

Inside the mess I found a cup of deliciously strong black coffee, but I couldn't find the Devonshire tea that was reputedly on offer. Later, I wished that I'd sent myself a postcard. It would have been a pleasing reminder of my adventure, arriving months later when I'd returned to the mundane routine of life. After our refreshments we made our way back to the beach to wait for our return Zodiac. I'm not sure what happened to Helen – I never saw her again. I was unhappy that I hadn't seen my redpoll, and rather resentful that I hadn't been permitted to look for it. However, I knew that I wasn't the first Australian birder to go home from Macquarie Island disappointed at the lack of a redpoll.

I stood on the beach and saw that at the water's edge Dave was gesticulating to someone behind my back. I turned around to see who it was, but there was no one there. He was gesturing to me. He wanted to know if I'd seen my redpoll.

'No,' I said simply, keeping all embellishments to myself.

'Well,' he announced resolutely, 'you're not leaving without it. This is your one chance in a lifetime.' With that, he gathered his son and the ranger who'd guided him around and took us all back up the slope to the tussock grass, habitat of the redpoll.

'I heard one,' I told him.

'Where did you hear it?'

We all spread out along the road around the spot where I'd heard the redpoll. Within five minutes I saw a small bird dart up from the grass, announce its presence and disappear into the tussocks, never to be seen again. It was just a silhouette. The birder's dilemma: can it be counted? I saw no red, no colours at all. I knew it was a redpoll – there was nothing else it could be. Lesser Redpolls and Common Starlings were the only passerines on the island at that time. Since the successful pest eradication, I believe Song Thrushes have been sighted and redpolls are now common. Back in 2009, going home without a redpoll was a real possibility. Could I count a colourless silhouette that didn't show itself properly?

'Well?' asked Dave.

'I'm just not sure,' I confessed. 'It must have been a redpoll, but I didn't really see.' My voice trailed off in disappointment.

Dave stood there, a statue of determination. I was not leaving Macquarie without my Lesser Redpoll. It was unthinkable. He simply willed that bird into existence. As if in answer to his willpower, one small Lesser Redpoll flew from the grass behind us, over our heads and into a tussock 100m away, calling all the time (no. 707). We all thought it was Christmas (well, it was, almost). The ranger looked at us benevolently. I think some people are actually envious when birders derive obvious deep pleasure from a simple sighting.

I should have hugged and kissed Dave and his son. Instead, I grinned and said 'Thank you.' Hardly adequate really. I was so elated, I wasn't upset that the Zodiac was too high in the water for me to get into comfortably. Nathan was driving it and he was, as ever, very helpful. So was everyone else, and I managed to get in without falling over or being yelled at.

There was some talk about deteriorating weather and the necessity of getting back to the *Enderby* as soon as possible. Nevertheless, Nathan steered our Zodiac around some rocks away from our vessel, where we admired a colony of Southern Rockhopper Penguins. I like all penguins (who doesn't?) but I have a special place in my heart for the milestone bird that became number 700. The seas swelled and it was very difficult to take photos from the bobbing Zodiac, so I sat there happily, just drinking in the birds. They were very endearing, doing what rockhoppers do, hopping (or more accurately jumping) over the rocks.

Everyone was back on board for a late lunch at 2 p.m. and the *Enderby* set course for Campbell Island. After lunch there was a lecture about photography in the dreaded lecture theatre. I could not consider leaving the bridge while we were in Australian waters and there was the remotest chance of seeing something new. So, I stood alone on the bridge and saw nothing new. My notebook records that I saw Grey-headed, Royal and Campbell's Albatrosses, and Black-bellied Storm Petrels. After the lecture a few others joined me and we saw Mottled, White-headed and Grey Petrels, and a Sooty Shearwater. Of course, all I really wanted was a Southern Fulmar.

For some reason there was a large crowd of people on the bridge that afternoon. An Italian birder at the far end of the room saw something interesting and pointed it out. From my distant viewpoint (and distorted expectation) I knew it must be my fulmar. I rushed across the room.

'Where?' I asked excitedly.

He pointed to the bird. It was a Macquarie Shag. As I so often do, I spoke without thinking, on this occasion unfortunately loudly: 'Who wants a shag?' I asked the crowded room.

2 Bruny Island

Bruny Island is famous among birders because it is the easiest spot in which to see all 12 Tasmanian endemics. Bruny has a resident population of around 700 people, and an area of 36,500ha, making it Tasmania's fourth largest island (the three larger islands are Flinders, King and Cape Barren).

KEY SPECIES
Tasmanian endemics:
- Tasmanian Nativehen
- Green Rosella
- Strong-billed Honeyeater
- Black-headed Honeyeater
- Yellow-throated Honeyeater
- Yellow Wattlebird
- Forty-spotted Pardalote
- Scrubtit
- Tasmanian Scrubwren
- Tasmanian Thornbill
- Black Currawong
- Dusky Robin

Also:
- Little Penguin
- Kelp Gull
- Crescent Honeyeater
- Forest Raven

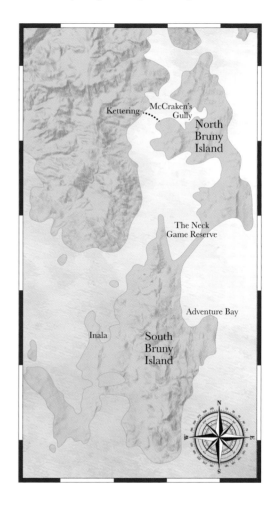

Right: Bruny Island.

The Kelp Gull was a lifer for me in 1994.

To get to Bruny Island, you take the ferry from Kettering, 40 minutes' drive south of Hobart. I saw a lifer from this ferry in 1994: a Kelp Gull. For many years I had struggled to see a Kelp Gull in my home state, Victoria. In those days we called the birds Dominican Gulls. They have expanded their range significantly and a trip to the Kettering ferry is no longer required to add them to your life list. In 1987 the *Atlas of Victorian Birds* described them as scarce. Today, I see them at Port Fairy whenever I do a pelagic trip there, and they breed on Phillip Island in Western Port Bay.

Back to Bruny: the island is in two distinct bits – the north, which is primarily agricultural, hilly and freehold, and the south, which includes state forest and some beautiful pristine bush. North Bruny is one-fifth the size of South Bruny. The two 'halves' are joined by a narrow isthmus called 'The Neck' – a great spot in which to look for Little Penguins after dark. Bruny is one of five islands nominated by the Australian Government's Threatened Species Strategy to eradicate feral cats – always a difficult task when there's a resident community. I wish them luck.

I visited Bruny to see the Forty-spotted Pardalote.

In 1994 I visited Bruny in order to see the Forty-spotted Pardalote. I remember this as one of the easiest ticks I've ever achieved. The birds were playing on a wooden gate at eye height on a bend in the road at McCracken's Gully. At the time I didn't realize how lucky I was. I've seen Forty-spotted Pardalotes a few times since, but never as easily as I did on that first occasion in 1994. They are rarely at eye height – but more often very high in the canopy of Manna Gums, where they are difficult to discern from other pardalotes. Both Spotted and Striated Pardalotes can be present in the same locations as forty-spots.

A decade later, in June 2004, I stayed at Inala, a delightful cottage on Bruny. I remember a plantation of Brown Boronia being grown for essential oils for the perfume industry. It smelled wonderful. I believe that there were too few growers to make a viable industry and the crop is no longer grown.

There were Flame and Scarlet Robins around the cottage when we arrived, and a Tasmanian Thornbill greeted us from a nearby gum tree. Tasmanian Native-

Tasmanian Nativehens grazed in the paddocks.

Green Rosellas were in the garden.

Crescent Honeyeaters, while not Tasmanian endemics, are easiest to see on the island state.

hens grazed in surrounding paddocks. Green Rosellas were in the garden, and I saw Yellow-throated Honeyeaters and Yellow Wattlebirds along the track. Black Currawongs flew overhead, cackling to draw attention to themselves. That was half the Tasmanian endemics in the first 30 minutes. The next bird I saw was a Crescent Honeyeater. These birds, while not Tasmanian endemics, are easier to see on the island state than on the mainland. Other such birds are Pink Robins, Beautiful Firetails and Forest Ravens. Alas, Lewin's Rail no longer qualifies – in the past it was easy to see in Tasmania, but this is no longer the case.

Dusky Robins were next to put in an appearance, then Scrubtits and lots of Tasmanian Scrubwrens. Then a Bassian Thrush, which, although not an endemic, did look larger than the Victorian birds. This is an example of Bergman's Rule, 'that, among the forms of a polytypic species, body size tends to be larger in cooler parts of the total range and smaller in the warmer parts' (from Ken Simpson's rendition of Bergman's Rule in his field guide). I saw a bumblebee and an albino wallaby. I

Pink Robins are easiest to see in Tasmania. This is a male.

This is a female Pink Robin.

The following morning I saw a Strong-billed Honeyeater.

found the botany interesting too. I admired Pink Heath, Mountain Blueberries and, although not a plant, pretty nevertheless, orange fungi. I learnt that the Blue Gums Captain Cook saw in Adventure Bay in 1777 are still there today, and that the grass trees on North Bruny are a thousand years old.

The following morning I saw Strong-billed Honeyeaters, failed in my quest for Forty-spotted Pardalotes and waded across two streams to investigate what I thought was a stranded moulting penguin. At that time anything other than a Little Penguin would have been a lifer for me. I must have been reasonably sure it was something interesting to take off my shoes and socks and wade through icy Tasmanian creeks in winter. When I approached the bird it got up and ran away, revealing itself to be a Pied Oystercatcher. Not much like a moulting penguin at all really.

That evening we went to the Neck Game Reserve in the hope of seeing Little Penguins. It was already dark when we arrived just before six. As we walked down the wet, slippery steps we could hear mews and brays from the colony. It was cold and the breakers thudded noisily on the beach. However, we only had to wait 15 minutes until a group of four penguins appeared at ten past six. They stood for a moment at the water's edge, gathering courage, then, single-mindedly, headed off in a hurry towards their burrows. I was happy. I'd seen my penguins. I was about to go home to my warm cottage when another determined penguin, all dressed up in his dinner suit, walked straight towards me. I stood statue still. The penguin walked right up to me, then around me as if I were some irritating inanimate object. Then another penguin followed. Then two more. I was thrilled. It's always a privilege to be accepted by the natural world. Elated, we drove home carefully, avoiding abundant wildlife.

The next morning the Black-headed Honeyeater was first to put in an appearance, the eleventh of the Tasmanian endemics. Now all I needed was the elusive pardalote that had been so ridiculously easy to see 10 years before. I could see tiny birds in the tops of the Manna Gums and I was sure that they were pardalotes, but what sort? The weather was cold and wet, and the light was not good. I saw some pardalotes lower down, but they were Striated. After much craning of our necks, Rog and I were both satisfied that we'd seen Forty-spotted Pardalotes high in the canopy. So that was all 12 endemics on Bruny. Some people do it in an afternoon. It had taken me two days. True, they were wet winter days, but it took two of them nevertheless.

Having seen all the birds I was free to visit the local museum, and very amusing it was too. I thought I'd learn about the history of the place – perhaps something about the biology and the botany. Instead I saw information about Sir Edmund Hillary, an old piano and a model of the *Kon Tiki*. Don't ask me why. I learnt that Matthew Flinders was related by marriage to Sir John Franklin, who in turn was related to Alfred Lord Tennyson. I'm always interested in anything about Sir John Franklin, because of his connection with John Gould. Franklin was Governor of Tasmania from 1836 to 1843, and the Goulds stayed at Government House during their visit. The Gould's seventh child, a boy, was born there on 6 May 1839. He was named Franklin Tasman.

Back at the cottage I sat on the verandah trying to photograph a pair of Flame Robins. The male robin said to me: 'How are you, are you? I'm very well.' Grey Fantails were very common and very friendly. I saw kestrels and Swamp Harriers, neither of which was on my Bruny Island bird list. I saw Black-faced Cormorants and a Peregrine Falcon – always an exciting sight.

I loved Bruny, and I loved Inala. When you go, be sure to make time for a visit to the local museum. You may choose to go to the Bruny Island Bird Festival, which is held every two years. This would be a great occasion to enjoy all Bruny has to offer with like-minded people.

I saw a Nankeen Kestrel, which wasn't on my Bruny Island bird list.

I also saw Black-faced Cormorants.

3 Three Hummock Island

In March 2002, a weekend on Three Hummock Island was arranged by the Bird Observers Club (which has since been amalgamated with Birds Australia, formerly the Royal Australasian Ornithologists Union, to form BirdLife Australia). Roger and I were eager to be a part of it, and I'm so pleased we were. The weekend was deemed an unqualified success by everyone present. Three Hummock Island was altogether captivating. The weather was great, the views were beautiful and the walks exhilarating – best of all, the birding was terrific.

KEY SPECIES

- Cape Barren Goose
- Little Penguin
- Short-tailed Shearwater
- Hooded Dotterel

- Wedge-tailed Eagle (Tasmanian race)
- Green Rosella
- Black-headed Honeyeater

- Tasmanian Scrubwren
- Black Currawong
- Forest Raven
- Dusky Robin

AUSTRALIA

THREE HUMMOCK ISLAND

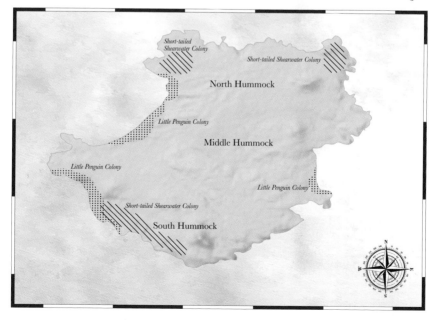

Right: Three Hummock Island from the air.

Three Hummock Island is part of the Hunter Group of islands on the north-west tip of Tasmania. It comprises 7,400ha of wilderness, and has a circumference of 55km. The coastline varies between exposed granite outcrops, sandy dunes and beaches. Today, there is no sign of the sheep and cattle that used to be present. Sadly, there is other evidence of human intrusion – cats, rats, mice, peacocks, Belladonna Lilies and thistles. The thistles at least have one redeeming feature: they are popular with European Goldfinches, which, you have to agree, are pretty, even if they don't belong there. We saw hundreds of them. The island is now a nature reserve and every effort is being made to eradicate the pests (I suspect this proposed eradication programme does not include the goldfinches). It has been suggested that access to the island should be restricted and visitors be required to apply for a permit, but there's not much point in such regulations unless there's some way of enforcing them.

In 2002 just eight people accepted the invitation to spend a weekend on this remote Bass Strait island. Our host, Rob Alliston, at that time the sole inhabitant of the island, knew every tree, every orchid, every blade of grass. The island's bird list had 82 species – we planned to see as many as possible. Unfortunately, Orange-bellied Parrots had been deleted from the list as they hadn't been seen since 1990.

It was a short flight from Lilydale (east of Melbourne) to Three Hummock Island. As we flew in we could see the three hills that give the island its name: North Hummock (160m), Middle Hummock (100m) and the highest, South Hummock (237m). They form a crescent halfway around the island from north-east to south-west, leaving a broad, flat plain in the middle. This is the location of the island's wetlands.

We arrived just before 10 a.m. and all chose to walk the 8km from the airstrip to the lodge where we would be staying. Along the way we remarked on the variety of habitats we crossed – heathlands, *Melaleuca* scrub, open eucalypt forest. New Holland Honeyeaters quickly made us feel at home, as did Grey Fantails.

Then the Tasmanian birds reminded us that we were not at home. Black Currawongs flew overhead, and we had a good look at a Black-headed Honeyeater. Fat Green Rosellas squawked as they flew past. Forest Ravens, too, while not strictly endemic, do have a Tasmanian feel about them. It's always reassuring to visit a place where you don't have to worry about identifying the corvids. Forest Ravens are the only corvids in Tasmania. We had lovely views of a male Flame Robin, then a pair of Scarlet Robins, then a couple of Dusky Robins. This last was, surprisingly, an addition to the island's bird list. A Yellow-tailed Black Cockatoo perched on the tippy-top of a *Melaleuca* and swore at us, distracting us from the Olive Whistler on

European Goldfinches are pretty, but exotic.

New Holland Honeyeaters quickly made us feel at home.

Forest Ravens are the only corvids in Tasmania.

the ground below. Plump Brush Bronzewings on the track ahead flew away noisily, and Tasmanian Scrubwrens hopped (appropriately) into the scrub.

Five hundred Cape Barren Geese live on the island, sharing their grass with 600 Eastern Grey Kangaroos. They all look quite at home and there's nothing to indicate that either of these species is endemic. The geese were introduced in 1968 and the roos seven years later. The arrival of the roos was down to the Tasmanian Parks and Wildlife Service, which introduced six pairs to the island in 1975. We saw lots of kangaroos, but none of the pademelons native to the island. I wonder if the Tasmanian Parks and Wildlife Service is pleased with this outcome.

Little Penguins and Short-tailed Shearwaters breed on the island and they live together happily side by side. Penguin breeding had finished when we were there but a few moulting adults remained, the feather-strewn entrances to their burrows an obvious giveaway to their presence. Very bravely reaching his arm deep into a burrow, Rob extracted a shearwater chick to show us. He might just as well have encountered a Tiger Snake – they are very common in muttonbird burrows during the breeding season.

We had lovely views of a male Flame Robin.

There are about 130 Black-faced Cormorants.

Plump Brush Bronzewings were on the track ahead.

Feather-strewn entrances to penguin's burrows were an obvious giveaway to their presence.

The chick was a cute fat ball of grey fluff. Rob told us it had hatched on 23 December. These remarkable birds arrive at their breeding colony on the same day each year. In some years there is a variation of up to three days, but usually they all arrive on the same day. Then each female lays her single egg on the same day, and the chicks all hatch on the same day. Dates vary slightly between colonies, but within each colony there is extraordinary uniformity. In autumn the birds embark on their huge figure-of-eight migration around the Pacific, spending the Australian winter off the Aleutian Islands and returning in summer to breed in southern Australia. Nigel Brothers, in his most informative book *Tasmania's Offshore Islands: Seabirds and Other Natural Features*, informs us (very precisely) that there are 168,724 pairs of Short-tailed Shearwaters on Three Hummock Island.

One very common bird that always gives me pleasure is the Australasian Swamphen (formerly known as the Purple Swamphen, before that just as the Swamphen when Eastern and Western Swamphens were lumped together, and before that, believe it or not, as the Bald-Coot). I love these birds – I reckon they have personality plus. They were near the lodge, far away from any swamp (although there is a swamp on the island, where Black Swans breed each year). My Australasian Swamphens were walking unsteadily along the top of a boxthorn hedge, more than 2m above the ground. The attraction was evidently the tasty orange berries, which were apparently worth the prickly precarious promenade.

We saw a single White-throated Needletail and, on our way back from admiring ancient Aboriginal rock carvings, we saw several pairs of Hooded Dotterel. These birds are classified as Vulnerable and are always a joy to see. Nigel Brothers reports that there are 14 pairs, mainly on the west coast.

For me, the most exciting sighting was the Tasmanian Wedge-tailed Eagle (also Vulnerable). It is estimated that there are only 600 of these birds in existence. In 2002 the population was 500 and declining, the main threats being habitat loss and collision with wind turbines. Mitigation measures have since been put in place and the population is now considered stable.

Three Hummock Island has Pacific Gulls, but (as yet) no Kelp Gulls. There are both Pied and Sooty Oystercatchers, and a colony of 130 Black-faced Cormorants.

When we left the island we'd seen about half the birds on the official list and added two of our own: the Dusky Robin and Ruddy Turnstone. Three Hummock Island is not on the regular tourist route. In 2002 the accommodation was basic. We had to walk through the one bathroom that everyone shared to get to our bedroom. Conversely, we were captive in our room if someone decided to lock the bathroom door. However, there is accommodation available today and it sounds a great improvement on what was there in 2002. So, if you ever have the chance to visit Three Hummock Island, don't hesitate. It's worth a visit just to see the Hooded Dotterels – and there's always a chance of a Tasmanian Wedge-tailed Eagle.

A very common bird that always gives me pleasure is the Australasian Swamphen.

Walking along the beach we saw several pairs of Hooded Dotterels.

4 King Island

My memory of King Island is of cows and seaweed harvesting, of being amused by a gumboot-throwing competition and of being bemused at not being able to buy the famous local cheeses on the island. I was there in 1990. It's possible that things have changed. It was wet and stormy the whole time I was there. I remember being delighted at seeing King Island Scrubtits (Critically Endangered), and a huge flock of White-throated Needletails (no doubt explained by the storms). I saw wallabies, pademelons and echidnas, and 52 bird species. Masked Lapwings were common, as were Cape Barren Geese.

KEY SPECIES
- Cape Barren Goose
- California Quail
- Wild Turkey
- Common Pheasant
- Indian Peafowl
- Fairy Prion
- Double-banded Plover
- Hooded Dotterel
- Ruddy Turnstone
- Strong-billed Honeyeater
- Black-headed Honeyeater
- Yellow-throated Honeyeater
- Tasmanian Scrubwren
- Tasmanian Thornbill

Six endemic races:
- Green Rosella
- Yellow Wattlebird
- Scrubtit
- Brown Thornbill
- Black Currawong
- Dusky Robin

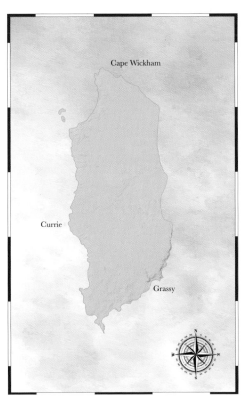

Right: A Cape Barren Goose.

Masked Lapwings were common.

King Island is named after Philip Gidley King, Governor of New South Wales from 1800 until 1806. At that time 'New South Wales' included Tasmania. Governor King learnt that the French explorer Baudin was leading a scientific expedition to Tasmania. King Island had not been claimed for the Crown, so King sent the *Cumberland* from Sydney to claim it for Britain. The *Cumberland* arrived just before Baudin in December 1802, and erected the British flag in a tree. Baudin sailed around the island and collected some specimens of King Island Emus, which he took back to France. The last one died in 1822. Today there is a skin in the Museum National d'Historie Naturelle in Paris, which is more than Australia has. The King Island Emu was last seen in the wild in 1805, and its extinction is thought to be due to seal hunters' dogs. Adult King Island Emus were black. They stood at 1.4m tall and weighed 23kg (compare this with the mainland Australian Emu, which stands at 1.5–1.9m and weights 35–50kg).

King Island has a population of 1,700 people and comprises an area of 1,100km², making it Australia's seventh largest island. Australia's tallest lighthouse was built at Cape Wickham on the north coast in 1861. This stands at an impressive 48m tall, or 157ft if you prefer, which is more than half the height of the central spire of

Melbourne's St Paul's Cathedral (and precisely half the height of London's Big Ben).

King Island is located in Bass Strait off the north-west tip of Tasmania, about halfway between Tasmania and the mainland. It therefore provides an important stopover for birds travelling between Tasmania and the mainland, such as Silvereyes, Grey Fantails and Flame Robins and, perhaps most notably, Orange-bellied Parrots (Critically Endangered). The parrots winter on the mainland and nest in southern Tasmania in summer. As I write, the wild population is estimated at 30 birds, but there are around another 400 captive-bred birds in various aviaries, which potentially could be added to the wild population.

A couple of special migratory waders call King Island home for part of their annual cycle. Ruddy Turnstones breed in the Arctic in the northern summer and spend the southern summer in the southern hemisphere. Some discerning individuals select King Island for their southern residence. Ruddy Turnstones like rocky shores with seaweed,

Silvereyes travelling between Tasmania and the mainland stopover on King Island.

Critically Endangered Orange-bellied Parrots winter on the mainland and breed in Tasmania.

King Island has more than its fair share of introduced birds, including European Greenfinches.

so King Island is the ideal choice. The other special migratory wader is the Double-banded Plover. It comes not from the northern hemisphere, but from New Zealand. This is the only wader in the world to undergo an east–west migration – and it's even more interesting than that. Some Double-banded Plovers never leave home. Only birds from the inland of the South Island of New Zealand visit Australia. Birds from the North Island and from coastal regions of the South Island stay in New Zealand.

King Island also has resident Red-capped Plovers, Hooded Dotterels (Vulnerable), a large colony of Short-tailed Shearwaters, Fairy Terns, Pacific Gulls and Black-faced Cormorants. Ten out of the 12 Tasmanian endemics breed on King Island. Those that don't are the Tasmanian Nativehen and Forty-spotted Pardalote. Those that do breed on the island are the Green Rosella, Tasmanian Scrubwren, Scrubtit, Tasmanian Thornbill, Yellow-throated, Strong-billed and Black-headed Honeyeaters, Yellow Wattlebird, Dusky Robin and Black Currawong. King Island boasts the northernmost breeding records of Yellow-throated Honeyeaters, as well as the southernmost breeding records of Golden-headed Cisticolas.

I was surprised to read that Fairy Prions breed on King Island. They nest in rock crevices or burrows, either in colonies or in single pairs. Little Penguins and Short-tailed Shearwaters nest in burrows on the island. Common Diving Petrels nest in burrows or tunnels up to 1.5m long, and pairs return to the same burrow year after year. Gulls, terns and oystercatchers all nest on the beach, and Black-faced Cormorants nest colonially on rocks. They construct a substantial nest of seaweed and driftwood, and usually lay two eggs.

King Island has six endemic subspecies, four of which have a threatened conservation classification. Both Yellow Wattlebirds and Dusky Robins have their own King Island races. Black Currawongs (Vulnerable) on King Island are slightly smaller than their Tasmanian relatives. Green Rosellas (Vulnerable) on King Island look the same as Tasmanian birds, but the taxonomists assure us that they are a different subspecies. Brown Thornbills (Critically Endangered) and the aforementioned Scrubtits are all difficult to identify LBJs (little brown jobs). Brown Thornbills are often in low vegetation, and Scrubtits are often in trees. King Island Scrubtits are slightly smaller than Tasmanian birds, with a narrower subterminal tail-band. I did not see Brown Thornbills and decided that was because they were probably extinct – at the time they had not been sighted since 1971. However, the birds were seen in 2002, then again in 2016, so a tiny population was around then. Let's hope they have a future.

Twitchers visit King Island for so-called 'plastic' ticks. These are introduced birds like Common Pheasants and Wild Turkeys. King Island really has more than its fair share of plastic ticks. As well as the pheasants and turkeys, there are Indian Peafowl, California Quail, Northern Mallards, Eurasian Skylarks, European Goldfinches, European Greenfinches, Common Starlings, Common Blackbirds and House Sparrows. With such a long list, it's amazing that there's room for any native birds.

When I wrote *Best 100 Birdwatching Sites in Australia*, King Island slotted in at number 95, which about sums it up. It is not among the very top birding sites in Australia, but certainly well worth a visit. Let's face it, anywhere in the top 100 sites in Australia is certainly worth visiting. The birder can expect some plastic ticks and some endemic subspecies, some rugged coasts and beautiful bucolic scenery.

Each autumn and spring the King Island Natural Resource Management Group (KINRMG) runs bird surveys on King Island, and BirdLife Australia calls for volunteers to help. They call it Wings on King and it started in autumn 2017. This would be a very enjoyable way to experience the birds of King Island in company with other birders. If you go at any other time of the year, the KINRMG would appreciate receiving your records. You can download a checklist from its website (www.birdsofkingisland. com/birds-to-identify), and post it to the address given there.

Some discerning Ruddy Turnstones spend summer on King Island.

Double-banded Plovers are the only waders to undertake an east–west migration.

I was surprised to learn that Fairy Prions breed on King Island.

5 Phillip Island

Phillip Island's penguins are Victoria's top regional tourist attraction, contributing an estimated A$400 million to the Victorian economy annually. Phillip Island is located in Western Port Bay, just 90 minutes' drive from Melbourne. Easy accessibility is just one of the island's many attractions. As well as the ever-popular penguin parade, there are cute, cuddly Koalas and lethargic fur seals.

KEY SPECIES
- Cape Barren Goose
- Little Penguin
- Short-tailed Shearwater
- Hooded Dotterel
- Far Eastern Curlew
- Fan-tailed Cuckoo

AUSTRALIA

PHILLIP ISLAND

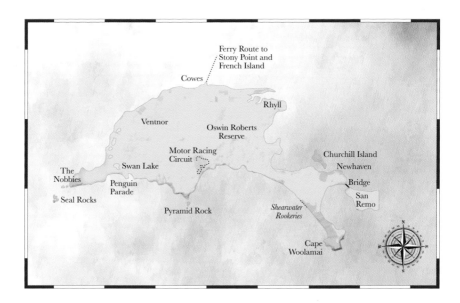

Ferry Route to
Stony Point and
French Island

Cowes

Rhyll

Ventnor

Oswin Roberts
Reserve

Motor Racing
Circuit

Churchill Island

Newhaven

The
Nobbies

Swan Lake

Penguin
Parade

Bridge

Seal Rocks

San
Remo

Pyramid Rock

*Shearwater
Rookeries*

Cape
Woolamai

Right: Phillip Island.

Kelp Gulls nest on Seal Rocks at the Nobbies.

Phillip Island may also, in fact, be a herpetologists' paradise: snakes are perhaps more plentiful than some people would wish – a fact not often mentioned in the tourist brochures. Moreover, believe it or not some people go to Phillip Island to watch motorbikes race around a track, and my hairdresser goes there to surf. I go for the birds. Apart from penguins there are waders, seabirds and bushbirds. I think of knots and curlews, swans and shearwaters, Kelp Gulls on Seal Rocks at the Nobbies, Cape Barren Geese in the paddocks and an aptly named, very restless Restless Flycatcher in the cemetery. One of my fondest memories of Phillip Island is of a Grey Fantail following me for the entire length of Lovers Walk. Another is of a Satin Flycatcher in the Oswin Roberts Reserve. Yet another is of a swamphen with its sweet black fluffy chick.

At 20km long and 10km wide, Phillip Island comprises 10,300ha and is Victoria's second largest island. It is linked to mainland Victoria by a bridge at San Remo. Here, every day at noon, pelicans are fed. Phillip Island has a resident population of about 10,000 people, rising to 40,000 in summer, plus a million Short-tailed Shearwaters. This is Australia's most abundant seabird, with a total population of 23 million birds. If you stroll along the boardwalk at Swan Lake in summer, you'll find yourself in the

A Grey Fantail accompanied me along the entire length of Lovers Walk.

Restless Flycatcher.

Satin Flycatcher in Oswin Roberts Reserve.

middle of a shearwater colony. It was a cute, fluffy shearwater chick that I'd admired on Three Hummock Island. These remarkable birds arrive on Phillip Island each year on 25 September. They raise their chicks, then leave in late April, flying 800km to the Aleutian Islands in Alaska, thereby enjoying two summers every year, one in each hemisphere. Shearwaters are sometimes called 'Muttonbirds', not because they taste like mutton: they don't. It's because early settlers ate them as a source of protein, that is, as a substitute for mutton.

Phillip Island is synonymous with the penguin parade and that is a marvellous magnet for tourists, attracting well over 700,000 visitors every year. Dressed up in their smart sartorial tuxedos, Little Penguins return every evening from a day's fishing at sea. They pause on the shore, waiting until a small group of them gathers, then together, gaining courage from each other, they hurry home up the beach to their burrows. They are the world's smallest penguin and arguably the cutest. They are certainly endearing, admired by almost everyone, not just birders. I find that watching Little Penguins gives me an uplifting thrill, like watching an eagle soar or

Pelicans are fed near the bridge at San Remo.

Australia's most abundant seabird is the Short-tailed Shearwater.

a Peregrine stoop. When I'm watching them I have to remind myself to breathe. In Australia we used to call them Fairy Penguins, and in New Zealand they're called Blue Penguins. I suppose 'Little Penguin' is appropriate, but it lacks a certain pizzazz. These darling little birds that do so much for the Victorian economy deserve a more alluring name.

One positive offshoot of the monetary value of penguins is the successful fox-eradication programme, which I'm sure would never have been attempted had there not been a demonstrable financial return. Fox control commenced in 1918, and in 1954 a bounty was introduced. In 1980 people realized that foxes were impacting the penguin colony, and control measures were intensified. But it wasn't until 2006 that the focus stepped up from control to eradication. The programme worked – no fox has been sighted on Phillip Island since August 2015.

One very special bird that you might see on Phillip Island is the Hooded Dotterel (Vulnerable). These birds nest on the beach – a very dangerous choice in twenty-first century Victoria. The Victorian population of Hooded Dotterels is 400 birds: not a very comfortable number.

Bar-tailed Godwits can be seen in summer at Observation Point.

I usually start my visits to Phillip Island with a stopover at Observation Point in Rhyll. Here I find that a spotting scope is very handy as I stand on the cliff admiring the waders below. In summer I see Far Eastern Curlews and Whimbrels, Red and Great Knots, Bar-tailed Godwits and Red-necked Stints. While I look down on the mudflats, honeyeaters, scrubwrens and silvereyes play nearby. Rosellas flash past and most likely a Willie Wagtail will sit on a fencepost and chatter to me.

There are plovers, both sorts of spoonbill and Little Wattlebirds on the island. While I'm admiring Crested Shriketits, kookaburras laugh at me. Brush Bronzewings are not rare birds, yet I do not see them every year. Phillip Island is a good place to add them to my annual list. I could say exactly the same thing about Grey Currawongs. Raptors include kestrels, Black-shouldered Kites, Swamp Harriers and Australian Hobbies. Exotic interlopers include thousands and thousands of Common Starlings, as well as House Sparrows, Eurasian Skylarks and very colourful if unwelcome European Goldfinches. Unfortunately there are also rabbits.

Raptors include the Black-shouldered Kite.

Because Phillip Island is so close to Melbourne I have visited it many times, but I have holidayed there just twice. Rog and I had a flat in Cowes in May 1975, and we enjoyed it so much that we returned again in November that year. As we drove home from that November holiday, my notes record that 'we stopped to listen to Mr Whitlam on the radio'. November 1975 was a dramatic time in Australian political life.

We saw a startling number of snakes – I recognized brown snakes and the Red-bellied Black Snake, but there were others I could not identify. I picked up cowries on the beach and admired bright orange starfish and Red Sea Anemones in the rock pools. I recorded mossies the size of blowflies and loved all the Koalas. Even in those days, there were great murmurations of starlings. Little Wattlebirds and Fan-tailed Cuckoos were common, as were White-faced Herons, which at that time I called Blue Cranes. We saw kestrels and Grey Goshawks, Eurasian Skylarks, Hooded Dotterels and Australian Shelducks (I called them Mountain Ducks in

1975). A dozen Far Eastern Curlews flew overhead and I admired oystercatchers, Pacific Gulls in adult and immature plumages, and (I believe my first) Horsfield's Bronze Cuckoo.

The things I did not record are perhaps as interesting as those that I did. I did not mention the Kelp Gull (which we used to call the Dominican Gull), although I believe there was a pair of these gulls nesting on Seal Rocks at that time. Likewise, I did not mention Cape Barren Geese. These geese were introduced to the Hunter Group of islands in Bass Strait in 1968, but I believe they were not on Phillip Island until later. I could easily miss one pair of Kelp Gulls, but it would be hard to overlook a paddock full of geese.

Apart from my avian friends, when I think of Phillip Island I picture pretty vistas with chicory kilns. I remember fog and unpleasant gale-force winds. It may be predictable, but always, the first thing I think of is penguins – which is predictable, but appropriate.

White-faced Herons were common.

I admired Pacific Gulls in full adult plumage.

It would be hard to overlook a paddock full of Cape Barren Geese.

6 French Island

I've visited French Island twice and on both occasions I was intent on seeing just one bird: the King Quail. The first occasion was a tour organized by the Bird Observers Club of Australia (BOCA) in October 2003; the second was a King Quail survey in May 2005. On the latter occasion the organizers had done a recce the week before and located a couple of quail. So we set off with high hopes. We walked all day, through difficult, dense heath and were rewarded with – absolutely nothing.

KEY SPECIES
• King Quail

AUSTRALIA

FRENCH ISLAND

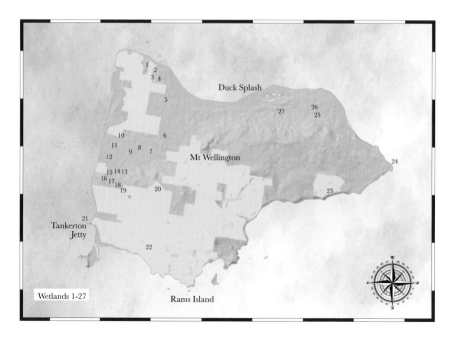

Duck Splash

Mt Wellington

Tankerton
Jetty

Wetlands 1-27

Rams Island

Right: Tortoise Head, French Island.

Strangely, the only birds I remember seeing in May 2005 were Eastern Spinebills, and we saw lots of those. King Quail like swampy heaths and dense, wet grassland. They are secretive and elusive, and can be difficult to see even when they are common – and they are not common on French Island. However, they have been seen every month of the year, even during severe droughts. Des Quinn and Geoff Lacey, in their book *Birds of French Island Wetlands*, state that King Quail are 'attracted to areas that have been recently burned, provided there is sufficient cover for shelter. The dark plumage of the bird ensures adequate camouflage.' It was actually Geoff Lacey who organized our King Quail survey. We were in good hands. The fact that we didn't see any of the birds just shows how hard they are to see.

There are perhaps 10 races of King Quail, distributed throughout Asia, New Guinea and coastal Australia. They are attractive birds and hence popular as cage birds. Ornithologists believe that escaped cage birds have interbred with the local Australian population. Nevertheless two races are recognized in Australia: one in the Kimberley and the Top End, and the other in a narrow strip down the east coast of the continent. Then there's the French Island population.

We saw lots of Eastern Spinebills.

I eventually saw King Quail at Malanda in Queensland in July 2008, so I haven't been back to French Island to look for them again. The funny thing is that I saw them in very tall grass, not in swampy heaths or dense, wet grassland. Here too I saw my first Eastern Grass Owl runs – beautiful neat tunnels through the tall grass.

French Island was named *Ile de Francoise* in April 1802 by Jacques Hamelin, captain of the *Naturaliste*, part of Baudin's scientific expedition. The name was subsequently anglicized to 'French Island'. Most Victorians know three things about French Island:

1. It is the only unincorporated piece of Victoria (that means there's no municipal council).

2. There used to be a prison farm on the island (it closed in 1975).

3. Koalas were introduced to the island when the authorities didn't know what to do with excess marsupials.

Not only is there no local council – there's no mains electricity, no mains water supply, no towns, no police. There's one general store and a post office. I remember lots of unregistered cars and an overall feeling of the Wild West. The island is generally flat and ideal for cycling, and bikes can be hired from the general store. The highest point is Mt Wellington at just under 100m, situated roughly in the middle of the island.

French Island is about 60km south-east of Melbourne. Located in Western Port Bay (which is, amusingly, east of Melbourne), the island is accessed by a daily ferry service from Stony Point (which is on the eastern side of the Mornington Peninsula, or from Cowes on Phillip Island). French Island is Victoria's biggest island. It is about 20km long and comprises 17,300ha, of which 70 per cent is national park. The resident population is a grand total of 60 individuals. There are 27 wetlands on the island, mainly freshwater, but a few saline.

With all those wetlands you'd expect lots of crakes, rails, bitterns, other waterbirds and Swamp Harriers. In fact there are three crakes (although Baillon's hasn't been seen for 20 years), two rails, lots of waterbirds and Swamp Harriers (classified as abundant). However, there is only one bittern: the Australasian Bittern. These birds are rare on French Island, but then they're rare everywhere. Their official conservation status is Endangered. The total Australian population in 2010 was estimated at 1,000 individuals and decreasing. The Victorian population was estimated to be 86–248 individuals. Their biggest threat is loss of habitat, so you'd think they'd flock to French Island. The trouble is that because there are so few of them, they don't flock anywhere. In any case, they are a solitary species.

'Why aren't Australian Painted-snipe on the list?' I hear you ask. Perhaps French Island's wetlands are too permanent. Australian Painted-snipe prefer shallow, vegetated, temporary or infrequently filled wetlands.

French Island has a bird list of 244 species, which includes 23 birds not seen for 20 years, as well as 10 vagrants. Apart from the King Quail (which is classified as Uncommon) perhaps the most sought-after species are the Orange-bellied Parrot (Critically Endangered, and classified as a rare winter migrant on French Island), Lewin's Rail (also Uncommon), and the Swift Parrot (Endangered and another rare winter migrant). Sadly, Orange-bellied Parrots are now so rare that no one would go to French Island to look for them. They are best seen at their breeding grounds at Melaleuca in Tasmania in summer. If you are exceptionally lucky, you may spot one at Werribee's Western Treatment Plant in Victoria in winter.

I saw 49 species on my BOCA tour of French Island, among them both Caspian and Fairy Terns, but not Greater Crested, which are supposedly common. I saw Scarlet Robins and White-fronted Chats. I was very surprised that we didn't look for King Quail, which I regarded as the island's specialty. I have two outstanding memories of that day: two beautiful splotchy Pied Oystercatcher eggs on the beach (which we were very careful not to tread on), and a flock of about 60 Far Eastern Curlews flying over as we sat on the rocks eating lunch. I've seen big flocks of curlews up north, but this was the biggest I've ever seen in Victoria.

We saw Caspian Terns on our BOCA tour of French Island.

I saw White-fronted Chats the first time I visited French Island.

Two beautiful splotchy Pied Oystercatcher eggs on the beach.

A large flock of Far Eastern Curlews flew over as we were having lunch on the beach.

We were told that there were no Superb Fairywrens on the island – a surprising omission as these birds are widespread in Victoria and occupy a large variety of habitats, from swamps and gardens, to open forest and rainforest, and they certainly like the coast. French Island could easily satisfy their habitat requirements. I didn't see any on either of my visits, but they are on the bird list as rare resident breeders.

Several good birds are common on the island, including Little Penguins, Grey Currawongs, Brush Bronzewings, Blue-winged Parrots and Yellow-tailed Black Cockatoos. As well as the Eastern Spinebills that were so prolific when we were searching for quail, White-eared, Tawny-crowned and Crescent Honeyeaters are all common. Little Grassbirds are common resident breeders, as are Golden-headed Cisticolas. Latham's Snipe and Dusky Woodswallows are common summer visitors.

Birds classified as abundant that we did not see included Short-tailed Shearwaters, White-faced Herons and Masked Lapwings. Shearwaters arrive on French Island in late September. The adults leave in April and the chicks depart in May, so we were unlucky not to see them in October. Perhaps we'd have seen them if we'd been at their burrows when they returned at night from a day's fishing at sea. However, missing out on the White-faced Herons and Masked Lapwings does seem pretty extraordinary. Some common birds we did not see included Stubble Quail, Blue-winged Parrots and

Golden-headed Cisticolas are common resident breeders on French Island.

Ruddy Turnstones. We didn't see Double-banded Plovers either, but we were there in October, so they'd probably all gone home to New Zealand by then.

I seem to see cuckoos much less frequently these days than I used to, so it was a pleasure to see Fan-tailed Cuckoos on French Island. In fact there are four cuckoos on the list. In addition to the Fantailed, they are: Pallid, Horsfield's Bronze and Shining Bronze. Cuckoos were much more common in my childhood.

French Island has a large colony of pelicans at Duck Splash on the north of the island. White-bellied Sea Eagles also breed on the island: the earliest record is from 1843.

Fairy Terns (Vulnerable) breed on the beach at Rams Island off the south coast. I remember being most impressed when our BOCA tour leader identified Fairy Terns by their jizz. I've always found differentiating between Fairy and Little Terns very difficult (sometimes impossible), so I asked her about it. She said: 'They just look like Fairy Terns.' I wish I could do that. If I can see the orange bill in breeding plumage, I'll recognize a Fairy Tern (Little Terns have a pale yellow bill, usually with a black tip). Out of breeding plumage, I've got no hope. I know that Little Terns are smaller but have longer legs, and that Fairy Terns are chunkier with shorter legs. I do wish I could look at a flock of wheeling terns and immediately identify them by their jizz.

I remember asking that great Melbourne birder, the late Fred Smith, how to tell the difference between Little and Fairy Terns. He seemed astonished that I could have any difficulty. He said that Little Terns have a black mark through the eye to the bill and a sharp white eyebrow. Easy. I felt a dill for asking and didn't admit that I was unable to see whether or not any small tern has a sharp white eyebrow.

The Lesser Sand Plover (Endangered) visits French Island in summer, although it is uncommon. There are quite a few Vulnerable birds too. There are our own Hooded Dotterels and some northern hemisphere summer visitors: Greater Sand Plover, Bar-tailed Godwit, Far Eastern Curlew, Great Knot, Red Knot and Curlew Sandpiper. Several birds that are classified as Near Threatened occur on French Island. They are the Blue-billed Duck, Flame Robin and the summer waders visiting from the northern hemisphere – the Black-tailed Godwit, Whimbrel, Grey-tailed Tattler and Ruddy Turnstone.

While I visited French Island with only one bird in mind (a bird I did not see), it has quite an interesting bird list – and not just of waterbirds, but also of waders and bushbirds, raptors and seabirds. French Island is a taste of something quite different and well worth a visit.

Fairy Terns breed on the beach at Rams Island.

The earliest record of White-bellied Sea Eagle on the island is 1843.

7 Kangaroo Island

We used to divide Western Whipbirds into four races, but the Western Australian birds have now been split from the South Australian birds. There are two Western Australian races, now called Black-throated Whipbirds, and two South Australian races, now known as White-bellied Whipbirds. All four birds are notoriously difficult to see. You can hear them easily enough, but seeing them is quite a different matter. By far the easiest one to see is the one on Kangaroo Island.

KEY SPECIES

Thirteen endemic races:
- Bush Stone-curlew
- Glossy Black Cockatoo
- Crimson Rosella
- Southern Emu-wren
- New Holland Honeyeater
- Brown-headed Honeyeater
- White-eared Honeyeater
- Red Wattlebird
- Purple-gaped Honeyeater
- Shy Heathwren
- Brown Thornbill
- White-bellied Whipbird
- Grey Currawong

Also:
- Cape Barren Goose
- Crescent Honeyeater
- Silvereye
- Beautiful Firetail

AUSTRALIA

KANGAROO ISLAND

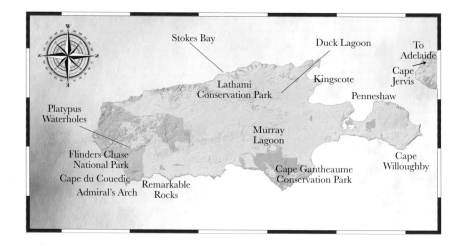

Right: Stokes Bay, Kangaroo Island.

I visited Kangaroo Island in August 2004 with the primary purpose of seeing what is now called a White-bellied Whipbird. Roger and I put our car on the ferry at Cape Jervis on the tip of the Fleurieu Peninsula, 108km south of Adelaide. We left at noon and arrived at Penneshaw at 12.45 p.m. We had intended an earlier departure but the 10 a.m. ferry had been cancelled because of 'routine maintenance'. The ferry we were on was certainly well maintained: we had a delightfully smooth ride, though I have heard that this crossing can be quite rough. Unfortunately we saw no seabirds – perhaps the price of a smooth crossing. I thought that the ferry was expensive (A$276 for the car and two passengers). This was in 2004 – you can bet it costs more today. It might be cheaper to fly.

Kangaroo Island has more than 500km of coastline, including pristine white beaches and rugged cliffs. The population is about 4,400 people. It's about 155km from east to west and around 55km from north to south. At 4,500km², it is Australia's third largest island, and more than a third of it is protected in national parks or conservation areas. It was named by Matthew Flinders in March 1802, in recognition of the amount of fresh meat he obtained from the island. A month later Baudin explored the north coast in *Le Géographe*, and you'll notice some French names still in use there today. *Le Géographe* took some kangaroos back to Paris, where no doubt they were a popular attraction in the zoological gardens. While the kangaroos made it back alive, Baudin did not. He died of tuberculosis in Mauritius.

Australia's first lighthouse was built in 1851 at Cape Willoughby, the easternmost point of the island. Today you can stay in the lighthouse keeper's cottage. I visited the lighthouse near Admiral's Arch at Cape du Couedic – no doubt named by Baudin.

The island is famous for its wildlife – charming baby seals, sea lions and (of course) kangaroos. They are Western Grey Kangaroos, but most macropods on the island are Tammar Wallabies. Luckily there are no foxes or rabbits. In the 1920s Koalas and Platypuses were introduced to Flinders Chase National Park from the mainland. In 1997 a Koala-management programme was instigated to reduce the impact these introduced animals were having on the native vegetation. Cape Barren Geese were introduced too, and they do look quite at home now. However, I can't help wondering what intellectual genius decided that Cape Barren Geese should be part of the Kangaroo Island experience rather than say, for example, the Cape Barren experience.

I expected a great wildlife experience on Kangaroo Island, and I wasn't disappointed. What I didn't expect was the flowers – both magnificent orchids and very pretty Cup Gum flowers. These latter blossoms featured on the logo for the

All the kangaroos on Kangaroo Island are Western Grey Kangaroos.

Cape Barren Geese were introduced to the island but they look quite at home now.

Unexpectedly spectacular orchids included this Gnat Orchid.

wilderness retreat where we were staying. Cup Gums *Eucalyptus cosmophylla* occur not only on Kangaroo Island, but also spill over to the Mt Lofty Ranges on the mainland. The (to me) totally unexpected and quite spectacular orchids included Gnat Orchids, spider orchids and several greenhoods. Many people know Kangaroo Island's iconic Admiral's Arch, but I found the orchids much more interesting.

A sign in the Visitor Information Centre boasted that Kangaroo Island had 14 endemic bird races, but unfortunately no one in the centre could tell me what they were. I managed to identify 13 endemic races, plus another four that occur on Kangaroo Island and the nearby Mt Lofty Ranges. I'm not sure how that fits in with the 14 endemic races the signwriter had in mind.

I already knew that the Kangaroo Island White-bellied Whipbird had a different call from other western whipbirds, and that the endangered endemic race of Glossy Black Cockatoo was a special attraction for twitchers. Effective conservation measures have upgraded the status of Glossy Blacks from Critically Endangered to Endangered, but there are still only about 300 birds. I heard them but did not see them.

Other endemic races on Kangaroo Island include Red Wattlebirds (which are slightly bigger than their mainland cousins), Bush Stone-curlews (which are smaller), Brown-headed Honeyeaters (which have a longer bill), White-eared Honeyeaters (which are darker), Shy Heathwrens (which have subtle differences in colour, striation and size) and Grey Currawongs (locally called Black-winged and very similar to the race on south-east mainland South Australia). Kangaroo Island Crimson Rosellas look like Victorian Crimson Rosellas to me. Other endemic Kangaroo Island races (that also look the same as mainland races to me) are New Holland Honeyeaters, Brown Thornbills and Southern Emu-wren. The local race of Purple-gaped Honeyeaters inhabits a wider range of habitats than mainland birds. I think of them as birds of the semi-arid interior – as there's not much semi-arid country on Kangaroo Island, I guess they have no choice but to inhabit woodland there. The four species with races that spill over on to the Mt Lofty Ranges are the Bassian Thrush, Crescent Honeyeater,

Red Wattlebirds are slightly bigger on Kangaroo Island than on the mainland.

On Kangaroo Island, Bush Stone-curlews are smaller than on the mainland.

White-eared Honeyeaters on Kangaroo Island are darker.

Brown-headed Honeyeaters have a longer bill on Kangaroo Island.

Brown Thornbills on Kangaroo Island look the same to me as those on the mainland.

The Kangaroo Island race of the Southern Emu-wren looks the same to me as mainland birds.

This applies to female Kangaroo Island Southern Emu-wrens as well as males.

On Kangaroo Island the Purple-gaped Honeyeaters occupy different habitats from those of mainland birds.

My bird hopped on to the track, revealing itself to be a Bassian Thrush.

Silvereye and Beautiful Firetail. The first three of these are easily seen on Kangaroo Island, but I'm afraid I dipped on the firetail.

As I say, I visited primarily to see the whipbird. I'd been told these birds were easily seen on the track from the car park to Remarkable Rocks, and it's true – I saw them there easily. But I'd seen them even before I arrived at the Remarkable Rocks car park. We drove from the ferry terminal in Penneshaw to our accommodation, the Kangaroo Island Wilderness Retreat, adjacent to Flinders Chase National Park. On arrival, the manager told me that he saw whipbirds regularly outside his office. I didn't unpack but went looking for whipbirds. Very soon I saw a brown bird skulking on the ground and my heart leapt. I stood quite still, not daring to breathe. My bird hopped on to the track, revealing itself to be – a Bassian Thrush. I walked on. Very shortly thereafter a bird flew across the track in front of me and landed in a bush, singing. Without doubt it was a White-bellied Whipbird. It flew up into a gum tree, then nearer to me into another eucalypt, making sure that there was absolutely no doubt about its identification. Then it flew away, never to be seen again.

The population of whipbirds on Kangaroo Island is estimated to be 2,000 individuals, which has absolutely nothing to do with how easy they are to see. Until

The baby seals steal your heart. This one's a New Zealand Fur Seal.

Kangaroo Island is a good place for Sooty Oystercatchers.

The island is also a good place to see Yellow-tailed Black Cockatoos.

these whipbirds were split there were four recognized races, and I'd seen three of them. Ironically, the one I hadn't seen (the Black-throated Whipbird that inhabits mallee in south-west Western Australia) is the most numerous and is the only one with a conservation classification of Least Concern.

Having ticked my whipbird I was free to relax and enjoy the pleasure of Kangaroo Island. Roger and I visited Flinders Chase National Park, 33,000ha of bush on the western end of the island. This is home to the photogenic Admiral's Arch (where the baby seals steal your heart) and Remarkable Rocks (where you'll see White-bellied Whipbirds run across the track).

We went on to Platypus Waterholes (surely these should be renamed 'Platypus Pools'). Here there's a 1.5km round walk with eight viewing platforms for watching Platypus. There'd been a fair bit of rain and the river was very high when we were there. The weather was gloomy and neither Platypus nor birds performed, although to compensate the wallabies were very friendly. It was, however, a very pleasant walk, and I thought that with a bit of sun the birds might be persuaded to show themselves.

Then we visited Stokes Bay, which, when we emerged from a virtual Aladdin's Cave, revealed a beautiful private sandy beach. Before we could get out of our car bus-loads of tourists arrived, so we didn't leave our car but moved on to Duck Lagoon. Everything was very wet and, at least in 2004, the roads were not well maintained. Even so, I managed a bird list of 74 species in one inclement day. Not altogether bad.

I'm told that if you visit Kangaroo Island in September, there's a good chance you may see Antarctic Terns. I haven't seen them here myself. It's also a good place for Hooded Dotterels, Sooty Oystercatchers, Tawny-crowned Honeyeaters and Yellow-tailed Black Cockatoos. Murray Lagoon in Cape Gantheaume Conservation Park (another French name) is reputedly a good spot for waterbirds, though I cannot confirm this as the access road was closed when I was there. Lathami Conservation Park is the place to look for Glossy Blacks. Nest boxes have been erected here for the cockatoos, but there was no sign of them when I was there in August and one nest box had been commandeered by Galahs. Perhaps visiting in the breeding season (April to June) might increase your chances of seeing these breathtakingly beautiful black cockatoos.

I know that I will never return to some islands featured in this book, but I am determined to revisit Kangaroo Island – notwithstanding the outrageous ferry charges. It's a wonderful place, and I'd like to see the Glossy Blacks and the Beautiful Firetails – and to see White-bellied Whipbirds again.

8 Rottnest Island

I don't remember how many times I've visited Rottnest Island. I do remember the first occasion in September 1982. Four things stand out in my memory, strangely, none of them birds. First, and most vividly, were the extremely cute Quokkas, second was my very limited success at attempting to ride a bike, third was a big crowd of extremely rowdy drunken football fans and fourth was the amazing spectacle of huge King's Skinks. This was the first time I'd encountered these enormous overgrown lizards.

KEY SPECIES

- Common Pheasant
- Indian Peafowl
- Little Ringed Plover
- Long-toed Stint
- Red-necked Phalarope
- Rock Parrot
- Singing Honeyeater
- Western Gerygone
- Red-capped Robin

AUSTRALIA

ROTTNEST ISLAND

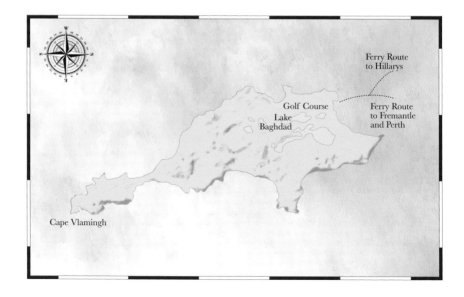

Right: Bridled Tern at Rottnest.

My first memory of Rottnest is the very cute Quokkas.

Rottnest is reputedly reliable for Red-necked Phalaropes.

Twitchers go to Rottnest Island to tick the Common Pheasant (look for it on the golf course). The island is also supposed to be reliable for the Red-necked Phalarope, Little Ringed Plover and Long-toed Stint. It is said to be an easy spot for the Banded Stilt and Wedge-tailed Shearwater, and the ubiquitous Sacred Kingfisher. Banded Lapwings are often seen at the airport.

In the past twitchers visited Rottnest to put Indian Peafowl on their lists, but an effort has been made to eradicate these birds from the island, and the self-important purists like to assert that the few males that remain are not tickable. Generally, to be tickable, populations should be breeding and persist for a decade (try telling that to someone who's just seen a Canada Goose on the Shoalhaven!). The Indian Peafowl on Rottnest have certainly been present for over a decade. They were introduced in about 1915. The fact that because of man's intervention they are no longer breeding does not mean that they are not tickable. How did these birds get there? They hatched there. You make up your own mind. I reckon you can tick them.

Rock Parrots used to be common on the island, but the population was decimated by cats and the aviary trade. Cats were removed from the island in 2002 and ornithologists are unsure why the population of Rock Parrots has not increased. They remain uncommon today.

Rottnest (Rat's nest) was named by a Dutchman, who thought the Quokkas looked like rats. His name was Willem de Vlamingh and he described Rottnest as 'a paradise on Earth'. He was on a rescue mission for survivors of the *Ridderschap van Holland*, a merchant ship owned by the Dutch East India Company that disappeared on a trip to Batavia in 1694. After naming Rottnest he sailed up the Swan River, reputedly the first

Banded Lapwings are often seen at the airport.

Rock Parrots remain uncommon.

Winter possibilities include Australasian Gannets.

European to do so, and named it after all the Black Swans he saw. He is remembered today in Cape Vlamingh at the West End of the island – incidentally a good spot to seawatch for petrels and gannets. Wedge-tailed Shearwaters breed here in summer, and it's a handy place to look for albatrosses in winter. Bridled Terns breed on the offshore stacks.

Rottnest lies in the Indian Ocean, 18km west of Fremantle. Ferries take you there from Perth, Fremantle and Hillarys Boat Harbour. You can see some good birds from the ferry. I recall seeing a Brown Skua on one occasion, so that must have been winter. Other winter possibilities include albatrosses, giant-petrels, Cape Petrels, Australasian Gannets and those darling little ballerinas of the sea, Wilson's Storm Petrels. In summer look out for Parasitic Jaegers.

Rottnest's 1,900ha boast a good bird list because it encompasses a variety of habitats. As well as beaches and rocky cliffs, there are salt-water and freshwater lakes, woodland, scrub and heathland. Most of the large trees have been cleared, but there is an endemic pine. There's lots of salt-tolerant shrubs and grasses. It is possible to hire a bike and ride from habitat to habitat. The salt lakes are often saltier than sea water and are home to brine shrimps, which attract migratory waders such as Red-necked Stints, Grey Plovers, Ruddy Turnstones and Curlew Sandpipers. As well as

The salt lakes attract Red-necked Avocets.

the migrants there are natives such as Banded Stilts, Red-capped Plovers, Red-necked Avocets and White-fronted Chats.

The beaches are good for Sanderlings and Pacific Reef Herons (we used to call these Eastern Reef Egrets). I remember failing in my efforts to see both Bridled and Roseate Terns. (I actually saw my first Bridled Terns on Penguin Island in Western Australia, catching the ferry from Rockingham. I saw the terns easily, then found a clutch of beautifully camouflaged Silver Gull's eggs and went back for my camera. However, the eggs so perfectly matched their surroundings that I couldn't relocate them so I came home without a photo.) On Rottnest, while I dipped on Bridled and Roseate Terns, I did see Caspian, Fairy and Greater Crested Terns.

Singing Honeyeaters are common on Rottnest. Thomas et al. in *The Complete Guide to Finding the Birds of Australia* state that Singing Honeyeaters 'on Rottnest Island are about 25% larger than mainland birds and are probably worth seeing in case they are split'. Singing Honeyeaters on Rottnest are not a separate race so they are unlikely to be split anytime soon. Johnstone and Storr state that Singing Honeyeaters are larger and darker in the south of Western Australia than in the north of the state or the arid interior. They make no special mention of the Singing Honeyeaters on Rottnest Island. The observation that Singing Honeyeaters on Rottnest are 25 per cent larger than they are on the mainland might simply be an example of Bergman's Rule (see page 37).

Several pairs of Eastern Ospreys are resident on Rottnest Island, and Australian Shelducks are abundant.

Interestingly, the Red-capped Robins on the island defend their territory all year round and have a different call from the familiar telephone call of mainland birds. Thomas et al. say that Western Gerygones on Rottnest also have different vocalizations from mainland birds.

One thing that intrigues me is the absence of Willie Wagtails on the island. Why should this be? They are present on nearby Garden Island. Why aren't they on Rottnest? Why are there no Grey Butcherbirds or Brush Bronzewings, for that matter?

There are lots of good reasons to go to Rottnest. The Quokkas are undeniably sweet, and even if you don't feel you can count the peacocks, the waders are certainly worth careful investigation, while the Singing Honeyeaters and Red-capped Robins are each interesting enough to justify a ferry ride.

Red-capped Robins on Rottnest Island have a different call from mainland birds.

9 Houtman Abrolhos Islands

Only once have I seen a lifer on the first of January. That was on 1 January 2008, when I saw the Lesser Noddy on the Houtman Abrolhos Islands. It was a great experience. In fact, I was surprised at how much I enjoyed the Houtman Abrolhos Islands.

KEY SPECIES
- Red-tailed Tropicbird
- Painted Buttonquail (local race)
- Brown Noddy
- Lesser Noddy
- Sooty Tern
- Roseate Tern

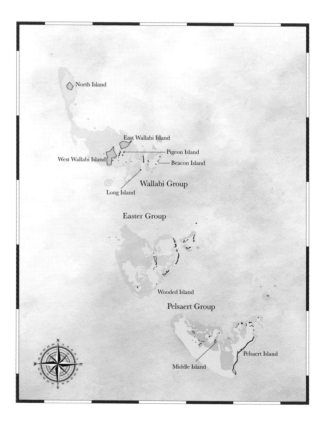

Right: The Abrolhos is an archipelago of 122 islands. This is Pelsaert Island.

I'd gone to the islands to see Lesser Noddies and Roseate Terns, and would have been quite satisfied with that. However, I also learnt about the history of the place, and saw an unbelievably large python, some very endearing wallabies, lots of other birds and some lazy yet intimidating sea lions. I found it very difficult to walk on the unstable coral and hated getting in and out of the dinghy, but I still loved the place. I travelled with Coates Tours. We took a bus from Perth to Geraldton, where we boarded a luxury catamaran that was to be home for the next three nights.

The Houtman Abrolhos Islands is an archipelago of 122 islands, 80km off the mid-west coast of Western Australia, spreading 100km from north to south. There are three main groups of islands: Wallabi, Easter and Pelsaert. In our short stay we visited all three groups. (Incidentally, why 'Wallabi' is spelt with an 'i' and not a 'y' is an enigma. John Gilbert, who collected for English naturalist and bird artist John Gould, travelled there in 1843 and spelt the name of the island with a 'y'.) Wallabies are present on these islands but not on others in the archipelago – or that was the case until a few years ago when some galoot introduced wallabies to North Island. It must have seemed like a good idea at the time.

Often referred to simply as 'the Abrolhos', these islands are one of two places in Australia with a Portuguese name. The other is Pedra Branca in Tasmania (this must be true, because I read it on Wikipedia). Pedra Branca (White Rock) is a big rock off western Tasmania, worth a visit for breeding Shy Albatrosses, Black-faced Cormorants, Australasian Gannets, Silver Gulls and Fairy Prions. Common Diving Petrels roost here but have not been recorded breeding.

Discovery of the Houtman Abrolhos archipelago is credited to Frederick de Houtman in 1619. He was captain of the *Dordrecht*, a ship owned by the Dutch East India Company. This is very early in Australia's history, just three years after Dirk Hartog first set foot on Western Australia, and it predates the arrival of the First Fleet by 169 years.

Just like the spelling of 'Wallabi' with an 'i', the derivation of the name 'abrolhos' is lost in the mists of time. Some say it is Portuguese for 'open the eyes' or 'keep your eyes open'. Others assert that it meant 'spiked obstruction' or 'offshore reef'. It is also said to be the call of the Portuguese lookout, which was adopted by sailors of all nationalities. Whatever the truth of the matter, it seems to be a warning to mariners of the existence of a reef.

If you do visit the Abrolhos, I recommend that before you go you spend some time in the maritime museum at Geraldton. Here you will learn about the two most famous Abrolhos shipwrecks: the *Batavia* in 1629, just a decade after Houtman discovered the archipelago, and the *Zeewijk* in 1727, almost a hundred years later. Both ships were Dutch and both ran aground on their maiden voyages. The *Batavia* is the second oldest shipwreck in Australia (the oldest is the English East India Company ship *Trial*, which was wrecked off north-west Western Australia in 1622).

The *Batavia*, under the command of Francisco Pelsaert, was on its way to buy spices from the Dutch East Indies, when two scoundrels on board plotted a mutiny. One was Jacobsz, the skipper, and the other a junior officer called Cornelisz. Jacobsz steered the *Batavia* away from the fleet. On 4 June 1629, the ship struck Morning Reef near Beacon Island. There were 322 people on board, 40 of whom drowned trying to get ashore. Those that did manage to get ashore were faced with the prospect of dying of thirst, because there was no water on the island. So Pelsaert set off in the longboat, leaving 268 survivors behind without any water. After 33 days at sea he reached Jakarta and was given a ship to return to rescue the other survivors. He arrived back at Beacon Island in September to discover that a bloody mutiny had occurred and 125 people had been slaughtered. Cornelisz had been in charge and had sent some soldiers under the command of Wiebbe Hayes to West Wallabi Island, ostensibly to look for water. Cornelisz abandoned them there. Wiebbe Hayes built a fort from limestone and coral, and improvised weapons from materials washed up from the wreck.

Pelsaert conducted a trial and executed the major offenders, while two lesser offenders were marooned on mainland Australia. Many years later, pale-skinned Aboriginals were said to be their descendants. Other offenders were taken back to Jakarta and tried again there. Pelsaert was held partly responsible and died a broken man shortly afterwards. Wiebbe Hayes was hailed as a hero.

About a hundred years later, in November 1726, the *Zeewijk* left the Netherlands bound for Jakarta with 208 seamen and soldiers on board. Captain Jan Steyns contravened orders and set sail for the land that Dirk Hartog had discovered in 1616. As a result of his disobedience he was shipwrecked on Half Moon Reef west of the Pelsaert Group. The first mate took the longboat and the 11 best seamen and set sail for Jakarta. They were never heard of again. The remaining survivors from the *Zeewijk* built a boat using material from the wrecked ship (not a bad effort) and sailed successfully for Batavia, reaching their destination on 30 April 1728. Six died on the way, but an impressive 82 survived.

In the past guano mining took place on the Abrolhos. Today, the main activity is lobster farming. Between mid-March and the end of June, 150 licensed fishermen live on 22 designated islands and add more than A$40 million to the state's economy.

There is also a thriving pearl industry. From time to time there's a proposal to construct a resort on one of the islands. So far, the lack of drinking water has stymied every proposal. Let's hope this continues to be the case.

The Abrolhos Islands accommodate the southernmost coral reef in the Indian Ocean. At these latitudes waters are generally too cold for coral, but the Abrolhos benefit from the Leeuwin Current, which flows from April to October. After the March full moon there is a spectacular mass coral spawning phenomenon. Add interesting fish to this colourful coral and the Abrolhos is a popular snorkelling destination.

There are 95 birds on the Abrolhos list. I saw 36 of them, or 37 if you count the Lesser Crested Tern (I believe I did see the Lesser Crested Tern, but this is well south of its accepted distribution so perhaps I did not). According to the Western Australian Department of Environment and Conservation, the Houtman Abrolhos archipelago is the most important seabird breeding area in the state. Seventeen species breed on Pelseart Island alone, totalling more than a million birds.

We left Geraldton at 6.40 a.m. on a Sunday and arrived at Long Island in the Wallabi Group at 10.15 that morning. There were 24 of us on board, including our tour leaders and the captain and his crew. To say it was a rough crossing doesn't really give a feeling of just how extremely uncomfortable and how very wet it was. Coates's advertising blurb stated: 'The sea crossing to the islands can be rough and lasts around 2–3 hours.' So we can't say we weren't warned. I know that at least two of us were seasick – perhaps there were more. Roger and I had taken medication, so we weren't ill – just drenched to the skin, unhappy and uncomfortable.

Did I see Lesser Crested Terns on the Abrolhos? This photo of Lesser Crested Terns with one Greater Crested was not taken there.

I was disappointed that there was no pink on the Roseate Terns.

The Bridled Tern, one of eight species of tern I definitely saw on the Abrolhos.

This was all soon forgotten when we walked around Long Island. Walking on coral is like walking on building rubble. Large chunks move under your feet with every step, so it was very slow going, for me anyway. We encountered sea lions lolling in the grass, Bridled Terns, Grey-tailed Tattlers and, a lifer I had come to see, Roseate Terns.

I'm always excited when I see a lifer. Rarely is there any disappointment. But I confess that I was just a little disappointed when I saw my first Roseate Tern. Pink is not my favourite colour, yet for some perverse reason I've always wanted to see flamingos, Roseate Spoonbills and Scarlet Ibis – and I'd always wanted to see a Roseate Tern. When I did, I couldn't see any pink blush at all. It was just another white tern. To notice the hint of pink I had to examine an adjacent pristine white tern, say a Greater Crested, then compare it to the Roseate. If I squinted and held my tongue in the corner of my mouth, I could just about persuade myself that the so-called 'Roseate' Terns were in fact very slightly pinkish – and the birds I was looking at were breeding, so presumably they were as roseate as they get.

After lunch we sailed for Turtle Cove, where we moored overnight. In the afternoon we went for a walk on East Wallabi and appreciated the pristine white sand, so easy to walk on after the mobile coral. We saw Sanderlings and White-browed Scrubwrens. There are 10 subspecies of White-browed Scrubwren recognized at the moment, and the Houtman Abrolhos race *balsoni* occurs on the Western Australian coast between Jurien Bay-Dongara and Shark Bay. This is a paler bird with a lightly striated breast.

On Monday morning the captain took us for what we were told would be 'an historic walk' on West Wallabi. For once, I managed to bite my tongue politely, although I was quite sure that the captain had in mind an historical walk, revealing some of the history of the place. In fact, it was historic too, at least for me. Again, we were walking on difficult unstable coral. We saw a dragon lizard and the biggest Carpet Python I've ever seen. We inspected the remains of the coral fort built by Wiebbe Hayes in 1629 – the first structure built by a European in Australia. We had wonderful views of Fairy Terns in breeding plumage (that even I could identify) and we saw sweet little Tammar Wallabies. The captain remarked that there was no fresh water on the island, and that the wallabies had adapted to drink sea water. Once again, I didn't challenge him, but I didn't believe him either. I thought it sounded like the sort of apocryphal nonsense that ill-informed guides dispense to gullible tourists. At home after the trip, I consulted my library and was surprised to learn that the captain was perfectly correct. Tammar Wallabies do drink sea water. I also learnt that Tammar Wallabies were the first Australian marsupials recorded by Europeans. So, for me, it was an historic walk.

On that 'historic walk' we also saw Caspian Terns, Brush Bronzewings and (most unusually) an Australian Raven. We noted that all the Pacific Reef Herons (we used to call them Eastern Reef Egrets) were grey-morph birds: there were no white morphs here. Unfortunately we did not see the endangered endemic race of Painted Button-quail that lives only on the Abrolhos. It's usually found on North Island, and East and West Wallabi. It has been recorded on Seagull and Pigeon in the Wallabi Group, but is not thought to be resident there. Although my 1998 edition of Johnstone and Storr records it as 'common', a concerted two-day survey in 2006 achieved just one sighting, and the 2010 *Action Plan* estimates the total population as fewer than 1,000 birds. The population on North Island could be declining because some bright spark introduced wallabies – probably the grandson of the genius who thought Cane Toads were a good idea.

Shearwaters on West Wallabi are very cooperative. The Little Shearwaters breed in winter; Wedge-tailed Shearwaters breed in summer. Thus it is possible for them to share the same burrows: the Little ones have gone before the Wedge-tailed ones move in. Very clever.

That afternoon we visited Beacon Island. This is where the *Batavia* survivors had clambered ashore. I was delighted to be told that it would be a dry landing, so I didn't have to step out of a heaving tender into swirling waves. In fact, although it was dry, I found it just as difficult. There were no handrails on the steps – nothing to hang on to at all. It wasn't elegant, but I managed, and I guess it was not as difficult as clambering ashore from a shipwreck. There were many crayfishermen's houses, although we were told that only one was occupied during the season (mid-March to June). We watched a pair of Bridled Terns feeding their fluffy brown chick. We really had some great tern sightings on this trip.

As our catamaran returned to Turtle Cove to celebrate New Year's Eve, we watched dolphins playing around us. I don't think anyone lasted till midnight. I was happy to retire at 9 p.m., looking forward to my lifer tomorrow.

New Year's Day was cloudy but my spirits were sunny as we approached Wooded Island in the Easter Group, and the Lesser Noddies that I'd come all this way to see. They did not let me down. There were thousands of them, sitting unexpectedly on healthy mangroves. In those days I was still using film, and Mr Kodak would have approved of the quantity I used.

The Lesser Noddies were unexpectedly sitting on healthy mangroves.

In the afternoon we visited Morley Island. Here the Lesser Noddies were sitting (as I'd expected) on denuded mangroves. The birds colonize one island until the vegetation is destroyed, then move en masse to another island and give the mangroves on the first island a chance to recover. We watched them sunbaking, most extending one wing only and enjoying the warmth. For the first time on the trip, it was in fact quite hot.

We tasted native grapes growing here. They were quite delicious – at once salty and sweet. They'd make a tasty addition to a salad.

Red-tailed Tropicbirds feature on the signs on Morley Island but the birds themselves are not common. I was delighted to see one: they are magnificent birds.

We moored overnight at Wooded Island, and in the morning found that our lights had attracted White-faced Storm Petrels to the boat. There were several sitting quietly on the deck. I'd never been so close to a storm petrel before. Their plumage was beautifully soft and the webbing between their toes was quite transparent.

The catamaran moved to Pelsaert Island, where there were huge colonies of both Sooty Terns and Brown Noddies. I had no trouble accepting the Western Australian Department of Environment and Conservation's statement that there were more than a million breeding seabirds on Pelsaert.

That afternoon we went for a walk looking for crakes and rails. Alas, we saw none. Again, I found the unstable coral very difficult to walk on. We saw both Lesser and Greater Sand Plovers, Bar-tailed Godwits and Great Knots.

I was delighted to see a Red-tailed Tropicbird.

It took three hours to travel back to Geraldton, where we spent the night before returning to Perth.

I'd gone primarily to tick Lesser Noddies. I'd seen them, of course, but I'd achieved so much more. I'd learnt about the history of the place, I'd seen Roseate Terns feeding their chicks, I'd learnt that Tammar Wallabies drink sea water. The birds were fantastic. My trip was historic. Without reservation, I'd encourage everyone to visit the Houtman Abrolhos Islands.

White-faced Storm Petrels were attracted to the lights on our boat.

There are over a million breeding seabirds on Pelsaert.

10 Cocos (Keeling) Islands

If I've been unlucky in my birding on some islands, it's been the exact opposite on the Cocos (Keeling) Islands. I've visited three times and achieved an impressive 23 lifers there, including such rarities as Von Schrenk's Bittern and the Tree Pipit.

KEY SPECIES
- Northern Pintail
- Eurasian Teal
- Green Junglefowl
- Barau's Petrel
- Von Schrenk's Bittern
- Black-crowned Night Heron
- Chinese Pond Heron
- Javan Pond Heron
- Western Reef Heron
- Chinese Sparrowhawk
- Buff-banded Rail (local race)
- White-breasted Waterhen
- Pin-tailed Snipe
- Red-necked Phalarope
- White Tern
- Saunders's Tern
- Asian Koel
- Hodgson's Hawk Cuckoo
- Common Kingfisher
- Drongo Cuckoo
- Brown Shrike
- Asian Brown Flycatcher
- Blue-and-white Flycatcher
- Red-throated Pipit
- Tree Pipit

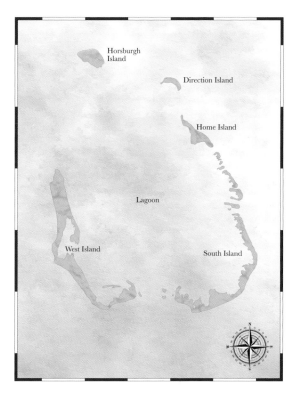

Right: The islands are picture-postcard coral cays, as this view from West Island shows.

Australia's Cocos Islands are officially known as Cocos (Keeling) Islands, to differentiate them from the Cocos Island off Costa Rica in the Pacific Ocean. They are located 2,700km north-north-west of Perth, right smack bang in the middle of the Indian Ocean. The islands are picture-postcard coral cays, with turquoise seas, white sandy beaches and your regulatory coconut palms. Average daily temperatures range between 24° C and 30° C. There are two coral atolls comprising 27 islands, but only two are inhabited. There are about 400 people of Malay descent living on Home Island and about half that number, mainly of European extraction, on West Island. There's a regular ferry service between the two islands.

The islands were discovered in 1609 by the English navigator William Keeling, but they were not settled until 1826, when John Clunies-Ross brought Malay labourers to Home Island to grow coconuts. The islands were formerly administered by Britain from Singapore, and transferred to Australian control in 1955. Birders are delighted that they were. Just like Macquarie Island, it is odd to consider this tiny outpost as part of Australia. It's thousands of kilometres from anywhere, with no historic, cultural or geographic connections to the Australian mainland – but birders wouldn't have it any other way.

The airport and the small European population are on West Island. The population on Home Island is descended from Clunies-Ross's fiefdom. John Clunies-Ross's grandson, George, constructed a mansion befitting his status on Home Island in 1887. Officially known as Oceania House and locally called the Big House, this two-storey dwelling is built from white glazed bricks imported from Scotland, and today is furnished with antiques. Birders go there because many vagrant birds turn up in the surrounding gardens.

There may be 27 islands but I've only visited six of them: West, Home, Horsburgh, South, Prison and Direction. On Horsburgh you can find the local race of the Buff-banded Rail and Christmas White-eye (Cocos Islands' only resident passerine). Birders go to South Island for Saunders's Tern. Prison Island is not recommended – it's just a miniscule dot in the sea, home to nothing but hermit crabs when I was there. Direction Island is of historical rather than ornithological interest. There's a pagoda there commemorating the *Emden,* a German light cruiser captured in 1914 by the Australian cruiser *Sydney,* not in fact on Direction Island, but off North Keeling.

North Keeling is 24km further north. This is the site of Australia's only record of Greater Flamingo (apart from fossils found in Lake Eyre), which occurred in 1988. Sadly, it is a place I will never visit, as access is by swimming only! Boats take you to the reef surrounding the island and you swim ashore from there. Not even a

Greater Flamingo could induce me to do that. The entire island is a national park (Pulu Keeling) and you cannot go there without being accompanied by a national park-approved guide.

On my first trip to the Cocos Islands, in February 2007, we flew from Perth via Christmas Island and it took seven weary hours of travelling to get there. It's much better to either fly directly from Perth to Cocos (which still takes four and a half hours), or spend a week birding on Christmas Island first and fly to Cocos from there (which only takes an hour and a half).

Today, birders go to the Cocos Islands for Green Junglefowl, Western Reef Herons and Saunders's Tern. On my first trip in 2007, neither Saunders's Terns nor Western Reef Herons had been accepted on the Australian list (both species were listed on the Supplementary List of the 2008 edition of Christidis and Boles, which basically meant that they were still under consideration by the authorities). At that time there was no path to the wetlands on West Island known as Bechat Besar. We struggled through the mud as far as we could. Others arrived at the water. I did not make it that far. Today, there is an easily traversed path. At these wetlands I've seen a Eurasian Teal, several Chinese Sparrowhawks and a Northern Pintail.

In 2007 we saw Western Reef Herons, but could not tick them until they'd been officially acknowledged. Saunders's Terns had recently been reported on Cocos, and while we were there Mike Carter turned up to confirm their identity. This he did, on a boat owned by the national parks service. We were not offered this luxury and were not quite sure where to go, had no knowledge of tides and consequent

Birders go to Cocos for Green Junglefowl.

At the wetlands on West Island, I've seen Eurasian Teal.

In 2007 we saw Western Reef Herons, but could not tick them until they'd been officially acknowledged.

There was a Northern Pintail at the wetlands too.

Today you are just about guaranteed to see Saunders's Tern.

tern behaviour, and had no access to boats. We did not see the terns. Today, if you go with Richard Baxter's Birding Tours Australia, you are just about guaranteed to see Saunders's Terns. He takes motorized outrigger canoes to South Island and celebrates with champagne after everyone has had their fill of Saunders's Terns. This was the reason I returned in 2014: just to see Saunders's Terns. I saw them on cue, then, just for laughs, saw another eight lifers as well.

When you arrive on West Island the first birds you'll see will probably be Green Junglefowl and White-breasted Waterhens, then White Terns. These must be the most beautiful terns, fluttering angelically in the blue, blue sky. On West Island, apart from Bechat Besar, birders visit the nearby farm, hoping for Watercock. This is where I saw a Brown Shrike in 2016, and (can you believe it?) a Square-tailed Drongo Cuckoo flew overhead and landed in a tree top just so that I could be sure of its identification.

Good birding is also to be had around the airport runway. I've lost count of how many Pin-tailed Snipe I've flushed here, and this is where I've seen both Red-throated and Tree Pipits. There's usually Oriental Pratincoles loafing at one end, and in 2016 a Von Schrenk's Bittern lurked in the tall grass past the weather station. Early in 2017 (when I wasn't present) a Barau's Petrel took up residence on the runway. Incredibly, presumably the same bird returned again in 2018.

Two other spots on West Island worth mentioning are the bottle dump (where I've seen the Red-necked Phalarope) and Trannies Beach (where, after some patience, a group of us had great views of an Asian Brown Flycatcher).

One of the first birds you'll see is the White-breasted Waterhen.

White Terns – beautiful, ethereal and angelic.   *I saw a Brown Shrike in 2016.*

Of my 23 Cocos lifers, seven were achieved on Home Island, five of them in the gardens around the Big House. In 2014, I saw Hodgson's Hawk Cuckoo and Asian Koels. In 2016, I saw the Blue-and-white Flycatcher, Black-crowned Night Heron and Eyebrowed Thrush. My Javan Pond Heron was in the coconut plantation and my Chinese Pond Heron involved a most uncomfortable wade through waist-high water across to Pulu Ampang. I did not enjoy this wade at all – in fact I could not have done it without the help of Steve Reynolds, whose beautiful photos help to illustrate this book. The wind itself was strong enough to blow me off my feet. There were sea cucumbers on the sea floor, a 2m sea slug, unstable rocks, sudden unexpected deep holes, coral and clams, huge intimidating moray eels, jumping mullets and even reef sharks. With each step I feared I'd fall over. But thanks to Steve, I made it and added the Chinese Pond Heron to my life list. Very bravely (or some might say stupidly) I waded these waters again in 2016, this time hoping for a Common Kingfisher that had been seen on the rocks. Alas, not by me.

The Cocos (Keeling) Islands are very pretty and would be worth a visit even without Saunders's Terns, White-breasted Waterhens and Western Reef Herons. I think the White Terns alone justify a visit. But it seems that each summer the vagrants keep getting better and better. I don't know why but each year more mega-rarities turn up. Who knows what will be present on my next trip?

A Drongo Cuckoo landed above so we could identify it.

Asian Brown Flycatcher at Trannies Beach.

This Black-crowned Night Heron was in the gardens at the Big House.

11 Christmas Island

It goes without saying that I love islands. Each island featured in this book has something special about it. However, Christmas Island (the one in the Indian Ocean, not the one in the Pacific, or indeed the tiny one off King Island in Bass Strait) stands out in my memory as a very special place indeed. The red crabs are phenomenal, the rainforest is magic and the birds are superb.

KEY SPECIES
- Red-billed Tropicbird
- Red-tailed Tropicbird
- White-tailed Tropicbird
- Golden Bosunbird
- Intermediate Egret (possible future split)
- Christmas Frigatebird
- Great Frigatebird
- Abbott's Booby
- Red-footed Booby
- Brown Goshawk (Christmas Island race sometimes called Variable Goshawk)
- Japanese Sparrowhawk
- Corn Crake
- Red Turtle Dove
- Common Emerald Dove
- Christmas Imperial Pigeon
- Oriental Cuckoo
- Northern Boobook
- Christmas Boobook
- Grey Nightjar
- Savanna Nightjar
- Glossy Swiftlet
- Cook's Swift
- House Swift
- Common Swift
- Barn Swallow
- Asian House Martin
- Red-rumped Swallow
- Christmas White-eye
- Island Thrush
- Java Sparrow
- Grey Wagtail

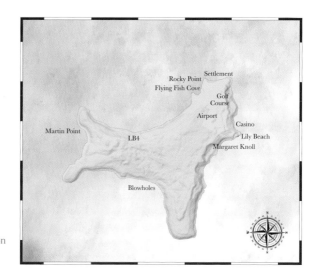

Right: Christmas Island.

I've been to Christmas Island four times and during these visits I've seen a total of 27 lifers. That's not bad for a tiny dot in the ocean that's just 130km² in size. That's one lifer for every 5 km². If I could do that on the mainland, I'd have 1,531,972 birds on my Australian list.

On my first trip to Christmas Island in December 2002, I saw all the endemics except the Christmas Boobook, which I managed to see on my second visit in March 2007. In November 2014, on my third visit, I saw a remarkable four lifers and most recently, in December 2016, I added an astonishing eight more birds to my life list.

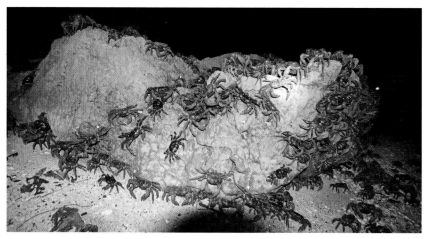

The red crabs are phenomenal.

The rainforest is magic.

Christmas Island is 1,400km north-west of the Australian mainland, but only 312km from Java. Planes unable to land on the island are often diverted to Jakarta, and visitors are always advised to take their passports. On my first trip, flying from Perth to Christmas Island, we were scheduled to leave ten minutes before noon and to arrive at Christmas Island at ten to four. There was some unexplained delay and we didn't take off until 5 p.m. The plane refuelled at Learmonth, then we were unexpectedly informed that we would be spending the night at Exmouth. We were put up at the Potshot Hotel Resort, which lived up to its name. It was Western Australia's answer to Fawlty Towers. We were given a room key and a map we couldn't read. A plane-load of people stumbled about in the dark, too tired to see the funny side of the situation. Of course the crew had first been shown to their rooms. We found our room at a quarter to two.

My advice to any birder wanting to go to Christmas Island is to go with Richard Baxter's Birding Tours Australia. My first trip in 2002 preceded Richard's tours: note that I did not see the owl. Unless you are as good a birder as Richard (which is highly unlikely), if you go alone you'll probably miss something you might otherwise have seen. Richard's tours encompass both Cocos and Christmas Islands on the same trip. Some tours do Cocos first, some do Christmas first. Thus, you either fly directly to Christmas from Perth (four hours), or from Cocos (one hour).

There are 133 birds on the Christmas Island list, but (thanks to Richard) I can add a few more to that – birds such as the Red Turtle Dove, House Swift, Common Swift, Cook's Swift, Grey Nightjar and (best of all) Corn Crake.

Taxonomists like to toy with our Christmas Island lists. The Christmas Island Hawk-Owl I had on my list in 2007 is now called the Christmas Boobook. The Emerald Dove I recorded in 2002 has been split from the mainland bird (now called the Pacific Emerald Dove) and the Christmas Island bird is now the Common Emerald Dove. The Christmas Island Goshawk I recorded as a race in 2002 was upgraded to a species called the Variable Goshawk in 2008. Amid great controversy, the bird was then lumped again in 2014 to be regarded as a race of the Brown Goshawk, where it sits (somewhat unhappily) today. The Glossy Swiftlet I recorded in 2002 is now bestowed species status by the IOC. Over the years taxonomists have had many doubts about this white-bellied swiftlet with a spotted tail, calling it variously the Linchi Swiftlet or Christmas Island Swiftlet. I'm happy to stick with simply Glossy Swiftlet, as long as I'm allowed to count it. Then there's the problem of the Oriental Cuckoo, which I've seen a couple of times. Both Himalayan and Oriental

The dove on Christmas Island is now called the Common Emerald Dove.

The Christmas Island Goshawk, once called the Variable Goshawk, is now considered a race of the Brown Goshawk by some authorities.

Cuckoos can occur on Christmas Island, and unless you happen to hear their call (and can identify it) they are impossible to tell apart. They rarely call away from their breeding grounds, so good luck with that.

I know many birders award a Bird of the Day for the most thrilling sighting of each day's birding. It's surprising how many different nominations there are when several birders have all enjoyed the same sightings. After a week of birding on Christmas Island we each nominate our Bird of the Trip. There'll always be someone who selects the Golden Bosunbird, and for very good reason too. This beautiful golden morph of the White-tailed Tropicbird is endemic to Christmas Island. You can't count it, it's not even a race, just a morph, but boy, it is breathtakingly beautiful. Every birder visiting Christmas Island must spend some time at the lookout above Flying Fish Cove, looking down on frigatebirds and Golden Bosunbirds wheeling below. I've heard two theories about the derivation of the name 'bosunbird', neither of them very persuasive to my mind. One is that it relates to the bird's high-pitched call, reminiscent of the bosun's whistle; the other that it relates to the bird's tail streamers, which supposedly resemble the bosun's marline-spike. ('Marline-spike: an iron tool tapering to a point, used to separate the strands of rope in splicing, as a lever in marling, etc.' *Oxford English Dictionary*, 2nd ed, 1991.) People sometimes refer to the Red-tailed Tropicbird as the Silver Bosunbird.

The Golden Bosunbird is always a favourite.

Every birder must visit the lookout above Flying Fish Cove.

Just for the record, my Birds of the Trips for my four visits to Christmas Island were:

- In 2002: Island Thrush, because I'd been writing about extinct races of this bird on Norfolk and Lord Howe Islands, and was delighted to see a living example.
- In 2007: Christmas Boobook, because I'd dipped on this bird on my first trip and had travelled to Christmas Island just to see it.
- In 2014: House Swift, because there were previously only two confirmed mainland records of House Swifts, one in Point Stuart in the Northern Territory in 1979, and the other in Caboolture in Queensland in 1994, and two confirmed records for Christmas Island, at the rubbish tip in November 2005 and in several locations in April 2008.
- In 2016: Corn Crake, because before we saw it there were only two, highly doubtful sightings of this bird, both before I was born, one in the nineteenth century (14 June 1893 in Randwick, New South Wales), and the other in the twentieth century (9 December 1944 on board a ship off Jurien Bay in Western Australia that had last docked in Melbourne). With just these two old dubious reports, this bird, which had not been sighted in Australia in my lifetime, had sat, unsighted, on my Australian list for 40 years, with no apparent hope of ever being seen. I was very surprised that I was the only birder present who selected the Corn Crake as my Bird of the Trip, although I must say that it did have extremely strong competition. That particular trip, in December 2016, witnessed more vagrants than any previous tour. Ever.

In 2002 the Island Thrush was my Bird of the Trip.

On my first visit the red crabs were migrating – all 45 million of them.

My first visit to Christmas Island was wonderful. The red crabs were migrating – all 45 million of them. The streets were a moving mass of red crabs. They were piled up in the doorways to the shops and cafes. They climbed over brick walls. And everywhere was the stench of dead crab. When we arrived on the island, on the short trip from the airport to our accommodation I saw seven lifers. They were (in the order I saw them): Christmas Imperial Pigeon, Christmas White-eye, Island Thrush, Red-footed Booby, Glossy Swiftlet, Christmas Frigatebird and Great Frigatebird. At that time I'd been birding for more than 40 years. There's nowhere else in Australia I could go and expect to see so many new birds in such a short time. I had a bird list of 32 on that trip, including 13 lifers, but not including the unidentified crake that walked around the nursery. Perhaps it was a Ruddy-breasted. I suspect it was but we will never know. I came home regretting the fact that I'd missed the owl and the waterhen, and couldn't count the crake. Such is human nature – instead of celebrating 13 new lifers, I regretted the ones that got away.

The first lifer I saw on my first visit to Christmas Island was the Christmas Imperial Pigeon.

The second was the Christmas White-eye.

I did it again on my second trip, although that was understandable as I'd only achieved one lifer – the owl. I should have celebrated this great sighting: it was, after all, what I'd gone there for. Instead I lamented the Savanna Nightjar that I'd heard but not seen. It is without doubt one of birding's most frustrating experiences – hearing but not seeing a target species. I often think I'd rather not know that the bird was present than to hear it, or even worse, glimpse it, and not be able to count it. I believe that some American birders count heards. Normal practice in

Australia is to require a sufficiently good sighting so the bird's identifiable features are recognizable – but then every birder has their own rules and standards, and what goes on a birder's list is strictly between that birder and their conscience.

I never learn. I did exactly the same thing again on my most recent trip. Not satisfied with a fantastic eight lifers, I came home regretting that I'd dipped on the Red-billed Tropicbird. I'd spent many hot hours in the noonday sun, standing in the exact spot where it had been seen the week before, checking out every tropicbird that flew overhead and looking for the one bird with a red bill. The tropicbirds go out to sea to feed in the mornings and return around lunchtime. The Red-tailed birds look chunky compared with the graceful White-tailed and Golden Bosunbirds. I'm told that the Red-billed looks quite different and that if I saw it there'd be no doubt about it. We were looking for speckled upper wings and back, but when birds are flying high overhead and you're looking up into the sun it is not easy to see the birds' backs. I could not have done more. I could not have looked harder or longer. There were lots of tropicbirds among the various frigatebirds, but there was no Red-billed. To find one Red-billed among 18,000 Golden Bosunbirds, 2,000 White-tailed and 2,800 Red-tailed, really is needle-in-a-haystack territory. I reckoned I earned that bird. Little wonder I came home lamenting its absence from my list.

Wherever you go on Christmas Island you'll find Island Thrushes, Christmas Imperial-Pigeons and kestrels. They are very common. The nursery just above the lookout that overlooks Flying Fish Cove is often a good spot for the Java Sparrow. I've seen Common Emerald Doves here, and this is where Grey Wagtails were hanging around in December 2016. This is also where the mystery crake was wandering about happily around my feet in the car park at dusk in December 2002. Alas, it has not put in an appearance on any of my subsequent trips.

The road to Martin Point is where birders go to see Abbott's Boobies on their nests. Gannets and Brown Boobies nest on the ground, as do Red-footed Boobies when there are no trees around. But Abbott's Boobies choose to nest high in the rainforest. If the chick falls out of the nest it doesn't have much of a future. In 2007 we picked up a bird that had fallen out of its nest and delivered it to be looked after by the national parks service. Richard has nicknamed this section of road 'Swift Alley', because when the winds are right it is a hot spot for swifts and swiftlets. Here I've seen Asian House Martins, Pacific Swifts, White-throated Needletails and (best of all) Common Swifts and Cook's Swifts. Thanks to the skilful photographers present, we were able to identify these last two swifts later from photographs (when I say 'we', I really mean Richard and other experts). Barn Swallows can be seen here too, or at the tip, or in Settlement. One memorable morning as I was eating breakfast on the balcony of our apartment block, Barn Swallows and Red-rumped Swallows flew overhead. I'd never have seen them if Richard hadn't pointed them out.

The nursery is a good spot for the Java Sparrow.

Here we saw a Grey Wagtail in 2016.

Richard Baxter with a rescued young Abbott's Booby.

Another advantage of going with Richard is that you get access to private property you may not otherwise be able to organize. A farm is being established with three large, most inviting dams. Here we saw a different race of Striated Heron *Butorides striata amurensis*, as well as Japanese Sparrowhawks.

I've walked the golf course hoping for snipe, but seen the Peregrine Falcon (race *calidus*) and Intermediate Egret (a possible future split). As well as the endemic owl, there are two nightjars, and recently a Northern Boobook has been seen (sadly, not by me). I've seen a Grey Nightjar once (in 2016) and heard the Savanna Nightjar twice (in 2007 and 2016).

Rocky Point is worth a visit – this is where we saw the Red Turtle Dove. It's also worth walking down to the Blowholes, although I found it difficult. It is a steep track with lots of small, loose stones, slippery moss and hundreds of fast-moving crabs scuttling under your feet. Naturally, it's always hot.

Birders also go to Lily Beach (for Red-footed and Brown Boobies, and Brown Noddies), Margaret Knoll (for boobies, frigatebirds and the view), LB4 (for Abbott's Boobies) and the casino (where the frigatebirds skim across the top of the swimming pool and where we spent a couple of very wet hours hoping that a Savanna Nightjar might appear).

Birders go to Margaret Knoll to see boobies and the view.

Every time I visit Christmas Island I have to relearn my frigatebird identification. I can remember that a black-and-white bird with a huge pink bill is a female Christmas Frigatebird, and that an all-black bird with or without a visible red gular sac is a male Great Frigatebird. I also manage to recognize a black bird with small white spurs on his armpits as a male Lesser Frigatebird. As to the rest, I haven't got a clue. Birds with orange heads are juveniles, but they could be Lesser, Great or Christmas. Male Christmas have a black head and breast, and a white belly with no spurs. I don't know why that's so hard to remember. Female Greats have a pale throat and female Lessers have a narrow white collar. It shouldn't be so hard and I guess if I saw them every day it wouldn't be. But I see them once every few years and my memory can't keep up.

Male Christmas Frigatebird.

Female Christmas Frigatebird.

The red crab migration is interesting to see. It occurs in summer, precisely when depending on the rainfall. Note, however, that if you visit Christmas Island during a crab migration some roads may be closed and you may not be able to access some birding spots.

Lest you fall into the trap of thinking there's nothing but red crabs and birds to attract you to Christmas Island, I should mention the blowholes, the rugged cliffs, pretty little isolated beaches, and magnificent rainforest with exceptionally pretty pandanus palms. Then there's interesting moths that swarm in the monsoon season, attractive toadstools that wear a netting skirt like a bride's veil, birdwing butterflies and huge nocturnal geckos.

If you're not expecting flying foxes, the first time you see them you may think they're birds, but you'll soon learn to identify them. Moreover, all the crabs aren't red. There are several species of crab. The red ones are phenomenal because of their sheer numbers and the Robber Crabs are phenomenal because of their sheer size.

I'm going back to Christmas Island again this year. Of course I'm hoping that some new rare migrant will turn up, or that the Northern Boobook will hang around until then. But even if that doesn't happen, Christmas Island is still a wonderful place to visit. I can always hope for a Watercock, or a Blue-winged Pitta or a Tiger Shrike. You never know what you'll encounter on Christmas Island.

The Robber Crabs are impressive because of their sheer size.

12 The Lacepedes

The Lacepedes are deemed important as a breeding site for Lesser Frigatebirds. But when I think of the Lacepedes I don't think of frigatebirds, I think of fluffy, inquisitive Brown Booby chicks. When I was there in 1999 there were lots of them and they were totally fearless. Mum and Dad must have been away collecting lunch and junior was left alone with nothing to do but await their return. So I guess my arrival was a highlight of a chick's morning.

KEY SPECIES

- Lesser Frigatebird
- Brown Booby
- Brown Noddy
- Roseate Tern

THE LACEPEDES

AUSTRALIA

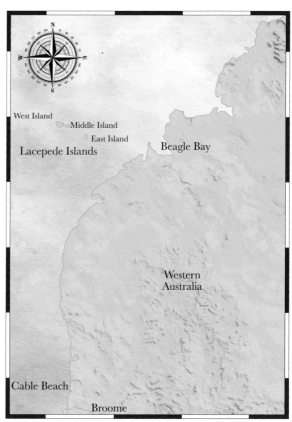

West Island

Middle Island

East Island

Lacepede Islands

Beagle Bay

Western Australia

Cable Beach

Broome

Right: The Lacepede Islands.

When I think of the Lacepedes I think of Brown Booby chicks.

I've visited the Lacepede Islands twice: once in July 1999 on our way back to Broome after a 10-day boat cruise up the Kimberley coast; and once in April 2014 on our return to Broome from Ashmore Reef.

The Lacepedes are about 120km north of Broome and about 30km from the Dampier Peninsula, separated from the mainland by the Lacepede Channel. There are three islands, predictably called West, Middle and East. They are treeless spits of sand and coral grit, comprising the Lacepedes Islands Nature Reserve, managed by the Western Australian Department of Parks and Wildlife, and covering in total around 180ha. Permission is required to land.

We've already encountered Nicolas Baudin, the leader of the early nineteenth-century French scientific expedition to Australia. We met him taking emus from King Island, then kangaroos from Kangaroo Island. It was a member of his expedition who named French Island (*Ile de Francoise*) in 1802. Baudin also named the Lacepedes (as well as Lacepede Bay in South Australia). The French naturalist Bernard Germain de Lacépède described several fish species. No doubt he was a luminary in his day, but if it wasn't for Baudin I venture to suggest that most Australians would never have heard his name.

In 1999, I visited Middle and West Islands. In 2014, I visited West Island. My memory is of huge numbers of both Green Turtles and Brown Boobies. In fact the Lacepedes are Western Australia's most important breeding place for Green Turtles. We attempted to count turtle tracks on West Island but gave up when we reached 300. The Lacepedes also accommodate the world's largest breeding colony of Brown Boobies – about 18,000 pairs. No wonder I remember lots of them.

Rats were eradicated from the Lacepedes in 1986 and the islands are once again a haven for nesting seabirds. BirdLife International has declared the Lacepedes an Important Bird Area (IBA), as more than 1 per cent of the world population of Brown Boobies and Roseate Terns nests here. They say there are 20,000 Roseate Terns. (BirdLife International is busy replacing IBAs with KBAs, Key Biodiversity Areas, so no doubt the Lacepedes will be transferred to this new jargon.)

I saw my first Roseate Terns on the Albrolhos in January 2008. Before that I'd looked for them unsuccessfully on Rottnest and Penguin Islands. In 1999, I was very keen to see one and hoped they might be present on the Lacepedes. If there are 20,000 of them breeding there it was not an unreasonable hope to see one. I was there in July, and Johnstone and Storr say that off the Kimberley Roseate Terns lay their eggs from mid-March to July.

The Lacepedes accommodate the world's largest colony of Brown Boobies - about 18,000 pairs.

One thing I've learnt about Roseate Terns is that they like variety. Some of them breed twice a year, others breed only once. Some are summer breeders, others prefer winter. They usually nest colonially, but single nests have been found. They never reuse an old nest. In Australia Roseate Terns nest on islands off Western Australia and Queensland. In Western Australia some colonies breed in spring and summer, and others in autumn and winter. In eastern Australia the main breeding season is from September to January. After breeding the birds disperse and no one knows where they go. Therefore while it was not an unreasonable hope to see a Roseate Tern in 1999, it was by no means a certainty. I was, in fact, disappointed. I did see them in 2014 on my return from Ashmore Reef, and in fact recorded them on 2 April, the very day we visited the Lacepedes. However, I saw them at sea and not on the Lacepedes.

I recorded 20 bird species on the Lacepedes in 2014. Brown Boobies were the most numerous (we reckoned 4,000). No doubt this is why Brown Boobies come to mind first when I think of the Lacepedes. Then come Brown Noddies (2,000), then Lesser Frigatebirds (1,800) and Silver Gulls (1,100). Unsurprisingly, these were the first four species I recorded in my notebook.

The fourth most common bird on the Lacepedes was the Silver Gull.

There were also several terns, egrets and waders. On the Lacepedes you can see both Pied and Sooty Oystercatchers. There are Pacific Reef Herons (we used to call them Eastern Reef Egrets), and as well as the abundant Brown Boobies there are Masked Boobies too. The terns include both Lesser and Greater Crested, and Bridled, and Brown Noddies. The waders include Grey-tailed Tattlers, Great Knots, Greater Sand Plovers and Ruddy Turnstones.

I remember that it was hot and noisy, but my most vivid memories of the Lacepedes are of Brown Booby chicks and Green Turtles.

Greater Crested Terns.

Bridled Terns.

13 Browse Island

As already mentioned (see page 7), there are three islands in this book on which I have not stepped foot. One of them is Browse Island, where I wasn't game to disembark because the seas were too rough. It is a nature reserve and a weather station, but access can be arranged through the Western Australian Department of Biodiversity, Conservation and Attractions.

KEY SPECIES
• Chinese Sparrowhawk

BROWSE ★
ISLAND

AUSTRALIA

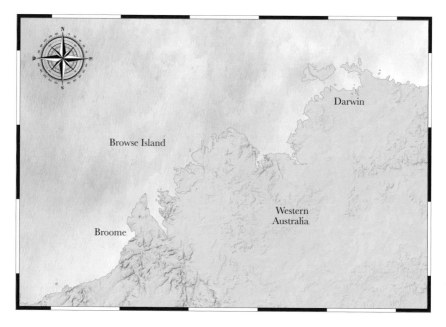

Right: Browse Island.

Our luxury catamaran *Reef Prince* moored at Browse Island on our way home from Ashmore Reef in November 2016. The island is located in the Timor Sea, 180km north-west of the Kimberley coast, and comprises about 17ha of sand dunes and limestone outcrops. I was up before 4 a.m., but couldn't wash my hair as planned because the boat was too mobile. I went downstairs for breakfast, then returned to my room to wait for the five o'clock departure of the tinnie (a small, open aluminium boat). By 4.50 p.m. I was tired of waiting and went down to see the first boat already departing with seven people on board. The seas were very rough and I was pleased to note that it was the captain driving the tinnie. He was

The whole place looked very dry.

always very helpful towards those of us who had difficulty disembarking. I did not know at that time that the island is surrounded by a reef, which sometimes makes reaching the shore challenging. When the tinnie returned for the second load, the captain announced that disembarking on the beach had been difficult: two people had fallen into the sea. Anyone unsure of their ability should not attempt to go. I am quite aware of my deficiencies so, reluctantly, I withdrew from the queue.

At that moment I just knew that there'd be some unbelievably exciting bird lurking on Browse, something never seen before, something that would make even non-birders marvel. If I hadn't waited in my room, if I'd gone downstairs as soon as I'd finished breakfast, I'd have been on the first tinnie. Other people had more confidence in themselves and the second dinghy soon took off.

I sat in the dining room nursing a cup of coffee and looking at Browse. It was not the most captivating island I'd ever seen. It wasn't large and was quite flat. The only structure I could see was a lighthouse, and the only vegetation apart from brown grass was some small shrubs. The whole place looked very dry, and didn't look very promising. I've since learnt that the vegetation is herbs, grasses, *Ipomoea* creepers, Indian Lantern Flower *Abutilon indicum* and Cardwell Cabbage *Scaevola taccada*.

I knew that those on last year's trip had seen an Island Monarch on Browse, a bird we'd just seen on Ashmore Reef. I hoped there were no other treasures I was missing. I sat watching people walking around on the island. They didn't look very excited. Bored, I walked on to the deck. Almost immediately I was hailed by two Indonesian natives in a canoe, who obviously wanted to get on board. 'I'm sick, missus,' said one of the most robust, healthy-looking young men I've ever seen. He grinned happily and his muscles rippled under his brown skin. I assured them that I'd get help and hurried off to inform the crew. After that I was not game to go back on deck again, so I sat staring at the island from the dining room.

I learnt later that Rohan Clarke on Browse had attempted to radio the boat to inform me that there was a pair of Chinese Sparrowhawks on the island. The radio didn't work, so I didn't get the message. When I learnt about it I was very grateful for Rohan's thoughtfulness, but much, much more, I was quite delighted because the Chinese Sparrowhawk was already on my life list. I'd seen it on Cocos in November 2014 (and was to see it again in December 2016). The only other birds they'd seen were Magpie-larks. So I'd made the right decision after all. I hadn't fallen into the sea and I hadn't missed out on a lifer. That's success in my book. We set sail for Broome at 8.45 a.m.

14 Ashmore Reef

On some island trips I've been exceptionally lucky to see a few extremely rare birds, including several never recorded before in Australia. However, on both my trips to Ashmore Reef I can't help feeling that I've been most unlucky.

KEY SPECIES

- Swinhoe's Storm Petrel
- Matsudaira's Storm Petrel
- Streaked Shearwater
- Hutton's Shearwater
- Bulwer's Petrel
- Jouanin's Petrel
- Black Bittern
- Lesser Frigatebird
- Abbott's Booby
- Masked Booby
- Red-footed Booby
- Brown Booby
- Oriental Plover
- Asian Dowitcher
- Grey-tailed Tattler
- Great Knot

- Red-necked Phalarope
- Brown Noddy
- Black Noddy
- Bridled Tern
- Sooty Tern
- Rose-crowned (Grey-capped) Fruit Dove
- Oriental Cuckoo
- Edible Nest Swiftlet
- Collared Kingfisher
- Arafura (Supertramp) Fantail
- Island Monarch
- Barn Swallow
- Arctic Warbler
- Yellow-browed Warbler

- Kamchatka Leaf Warbler
- Oriental Reed Warbler
- Middendorff's Grasshopper Warbler
- Pallas's Grasshopper Warbler
- Asian Brown Flycatcher
- Eastern Yellow Wagtail
- Grey Wagtail

ASHMORE REEF ★

AUSTRALIA

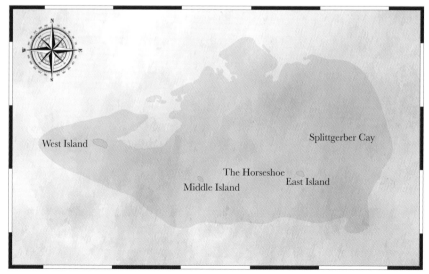

West Island

Splittgerber Cay

The Horseshoe

Middle Island

East Island

Right: Visitors spend most time on West Island.

I've visited Ashmore Reef once in autumn and once in spring. Spring records for Ashmore Reef go back 20 years, so birders know what exotic species might possibly turn up. The autumn trip was really a bit of an experiment. While there had been ornithological surveys in autumn, there hadn't been many, and before 2014 there'd been no commercial trips at all. No one really knew what might turn up in autumn. In fact, not much did, and I came home disappointed.

Sitting at home in my study before I'd ever travelled to Ashmore Reef, I expected that when I did, I'd see three storm petrels: Leach's, Swinhoe's and Matsudaira's. When I didn't see any on my autumn trip I learnt that they were only seen in spring. When I visited in spring I was told that all the early records of Leach's Storm Petrel were now regarded with scepticism. I did pick up Swinhoe's on that trip, but did not see Matsudaira's. At the time I was told that we were too late – it was November. We should have been there in October, it was said. Later I learnt that the boat had deviated from the set course and this was the probable explanation for missing out on Matsudaira's. These warm-water storm petrels are associated with cold-water convergences. They breed at any time between January and June on islands south of Japan, then disperse to the Seychelles. They are seen on most Ashmore Reef trips (17 out of 23). Since 2001 they'd been seen every spring except in 2016, the year I travelled. Rationally or not, I felt I'd been cheated.

I managed to see a Swinhoe's Storm Petrel on my second trip to Ashmore Reef.

Ashmore Reef is located 400 nautical miles west of Darwin and 90 nautical miles south of the Indonesian island of Roti. On both of my visits I travelled in the luxury catamaran *Reef Prince*, which took two and a half days to get to Ashmore Reef from Broome. The seas can be rough and medication is recommended.

The Ashmore Reef National Nature Reserve comprises an area of 583km², including three small islands and several shifting sand cays. The islands are ingeniously named East, Middle and West. Most time is spent on West Island, which at some 23ha is the largest of the three. We visited West Island twice each day, in the early morning and late afternoon. On my first visit we were not permitted to land on Middle Island because of a Red Fire Ant eradication programme. By my second visit the eradication programme had been abandoned and we were given permission to land. Red Fire Ants make life hard for Wedge-tailed Shearwater chicks and hatching baby Green Turtles, and I imagine any other creature that nests underground.

Trips to Ashmore Reef are organized by George Swann from Kimberley Birdwatching, based in Broome. The guides are usually Rohan Clarke and Mike Carter. On my first trip Rohan was replaced by Adrian Boyle.

My first trip to Ashmore started in Broome on Wednesday, 26 March 2014. A bus picked me up at my motel and cruised around town, apparently at random, picking up passengers in no apparent order. When it was full I assumed we'd head for the jetty, but we did not. We kept going and people kept getting on. Finally, a roll call revealed that one passenger was missing, so we retraced our steps and found him. By now, several people were standing in the bus. I suppose that's legal: commuters stand in buses every day. The bus drove us not to the jetty as I'd assumed, but to the beach. Here we were greeted with what to me was quite a surprise: the luxury catamaran was moored at sea and we had to access it by tinnie. We got to the tinnie by wading into the water (about waist deep as I recall) and somehow scrambling on to the dinghy. I did not think this was dignified. In fact, truth be known, I found it quite difficult. I don't like getting wet at any time, and intentionally wading into the sea is not something I'd ever do voluntarily. On this occasion it appeared that there was no option.

I put my binoculars in my backpack, gritted my teeth and set off. It seemed a long, wet walk and I was constantly buffeted by waves trying to knock me to my feet. They did their best. I concentrated on not falling over. An offensively pretty girl was waiting at the tinnie. Mistakenly, I imagined she was there to help us to get on to the boat. Looking back now I honestly don't think it occurred to anyone that any passenger could possibly require help to get on to a tinnie that was surging in the sea. The girl was there to show off her expensive orthodontic work, to welcome us and to give us a name tag. I kid you not. While I needed both hands to grab on to the moving tinnie, this alien creature thought the most important item on the agenda was for me to pin a name tag on to my T-shirt. It goes without saying that such a crucial activity could not possibly wait until we were aboard the *Reef Prince*.

The boat set sail at about 8.30 a.m. My notes record: 'Hutton's Shearwaters predominated in the morning and Streaked Shearwaters in the afternoon. Also saw Common Bottlenose, tiny Dwarf Spinner Dolphins and lots of flying fish.'

The next morning at 5.40 a.m. I saw my first lifer. It was a Bulwer's Petrel sitting on the water in front of the boat. We saw about 70 during the day. It was unpleasantly hot. An Abbott's Booby flew over the boat, checking us out. Later a customs plane did likewise.

Hutton's Shearwaters predominated in the morning.

Streaked Shearwaters were most noticeable in the afternoon.

An Abbott's Booby flew over the boat, checking us out.

The following day we saw an illegal Indonesian fishing boat and a floating drum called a fish-aggregating device (FAD). We were told that these devices were quite legal. They are man-made objects widely used to attract pelagic fish, which congregate around the buoys.

At lunchtime we arrived at West Island. The Navy gave us the OK and we went ashore after lunch. I wore brand-new sandals called Tivas, which were supposedly perfect for such conditions. Walking ashore from the dinghy, both my Tivas lost their soles. I did this walk barefoot from then on and carried sand shoes in my backpack. It was a long walk – about a kilometre through warm, shallow water. We saw Black-tipped Reef Sharks in the shallows, but they were no real threat. I remember the sea as quite benign. The walk was hot, tiring and tiresome, but in no way dangerous – and it certainly beat getting in and out of tinnies.

On that first day we stayed on West Island until 6 p.m., examining every bush for a rarity. We saw lots of Sacred Kingfishers, several Buff-banded Rails, one Oriental Reed Warbler and one Oriental Cuckoo. It was hot.

It was a long walk to the Reef Prince.

There were lots of Sacred Kingfishers.

Walking through spinifex, hoping to flush something rare.

The vegetation of West Island was mainly bushes, vines and grasses. There were two Coconut Palms, but otherwise no trees. There were large bushes around the perimeter, mainly Octopus Bush, but also Cardwell Cabbage tree and Fish Plate-bush. The Octopus Bush grows to 6m tall and has silvery fleshy leaves. Plants have either male or female flowers. The female flowers resemble the tentacles of an octopus, hence the common name. The middle of the island was covered with low, dense vines, creeping over the ground and intent on tripping me up with each step I took. There were night-flowering *Ipomoea* called Moon Flowers, a convolvulus creeper called Goat's Foot, a herb called Asthma Plant and lots of grasses including Buffel Grass and a couple of sorts of spinifex, one of which was extremely difficult to walk through – but we did several times each day, hoping to flush some rare vagrant, or to be truthful, the blokes did. I did it once, then decided I could be more helpful standing on the sideline, watching.

Each of the next three mornings saw us off to West Island before dawn, admiring the moon from the dinghy. On Saturday we saw the most exciting bird of the trip: a Yellow-browed Warbler. Not everyone had tickable views of it and the photos were far from perfect. In fact, it took a few days for the experts to satisfy themselves as to the bird's identity. We also saw Barn Swallows and a White-winged Triller. The next day there were no new birds on West Island, but we found several perfect dead baby turtles, victims of fire ants.

On Saturday we visited Middle Island and saw an ominous Tiger Shark beside the tinnie. I was surprised to see it in such shallow water. That really was something to be alarmed about. We were permitted to circumnavigate the island within a metre of the shore. As the island is quite flat and small, this gave excellent views of all the birds present. We certainly saw a lot of birds. The most numerous were 1,200 Brown Noddies, and hundreds of Lesser Frigatebirds, Brown Boobies, Greater Sand Plovers, Grey-tailed Tattlers, Ruddy Turnstones and Whimbrels.

On Sunday we took a very long and extremely uncomfortable, bumpy tinnie ride to East Island. I thought it was noddy heaven. There were 35,000 Brown Noddies nesting, 2,500 Black Noddies and 10–20 Lesser Noddies. Then to Splittgerber Cay, where we tolerated the heat in order to admire thousands of waders. The best were several Asian Dowitchers in full breeding plumage.

On Monday we headed back to Broome via the Lacepedes. Highlights of the day were a Jouanin's Petrel and a Red-necked Phalarope. The Jouanin's Petrel was a lifer for me, so it was particularly welcome. We were instructed to note the tapered tail, a diagnostic feature. I often have difficulty observing seabirds' quintessential features,

Noddy heaven.

such as the colour of a giant petrel's bill or the bill-to-head ratio of a shearwater. I'm delighted to report that I did observe the tapered tail of Jouanin's Petrel. Phalaropes are unusual long-necked waders that characteristically swim in small circles. I really hadn't expected to see one swimming around on the sea beside the boat. That just shows my ignorance: these birds are usually solitary, and spend most of their time alone at sea.

I was disappointed to leave Ashmore Reef with just three lifers under my belt, and couldn't wait to return in spring and rectify the situation. Conditions on the islands were frankly exhausting and I appreciated the air-conditioned splendour of the *Reef Prince*. Kimberley Birdwatching usually takes a less luxurious boat, *Flying Fish II*. I've never been on this boat but have spoken to several people who have. Different people are prepared to put up with different levels of discomfort in their birding exploits. As for myself, after a difficult day of clambering on and off heaving tinnies, wading through shark-infested seas and walking in extreme heat for hours over antagonistic terrain, I require a few comforts. I thought it might be some time before a boat of the standard of the *Reef Prince* would visit Ashmore Reef again, so I was delighted to learn that it was going again in 2016. I had read reports of the 2015 trip with evident envy. My mouth watered at thoughts of Middendorff's Grasshopper Warbler – the very name sounded excitingly exotic.

I compiled a wish list of eight species, all of which had been seen on Ashmore Reef on multiple occasions. I thought my list was modest and achievable. On it were Swinhoe's Storm Petrel; Matsudairas's Storm Petrel; Collared Kingfisher (a recent split from the bird found on mainland Australia, previously known by this name and now called a Torresian Kingfisher); Grey Wagtail; Asian Brown Flycatcher; Arctic Warbler; Middendorff's Grasshopper Warbler and Island Monarch. I ran my list past a couple of knowledgeable experts and was overjoyed with anticipation when the general consensus was that my wishes were not extravagant and might well be fulfilled. So that was my public wish list. Secretly, I hoped for more. How about a Pallas's Grasshopper Warbler or a Kamchatka Leaf Warbler? I learnt that grasshopper warblers skulk on the ground and leaf warblers hide among the leaves at eye height. I was ready for some very exciting birds.

On Wednesday, 2 November 2016, George picked me up from my motel at a quarter to six. He gathered a couple more passengers and drove us to Entrance Point. The tinnie came close to shore and we barely got our feet wet as we stepped on board – quite a contrast to my previous experience. However, the ease in getting on to the tinnie was not mirrored in getting off it and on to the *Reef Prince*. Clambering over the front of the tinnie, then managing a very big step down on to the catamaran, was neither easy nor elegant.

On the *Reef Prince* we were welcomed and instructed to drink Gaterade. The water on board is all desalinated sea water, so all the salts have been removed. The importance of replacing these salts for the sake of our health was impressed upon us. I don't like the taste of Gaterade but was quite happy to swallow my medicine with a smile. It was a small price to pay for all the great birds I was going to see. Shade cloth had been erected over the seats on the bow and I sat enjoying the view as we set sail for Ashmore Reef. I sought advice about taking Travacalm, decided I'd be fine without it and soon regretted my decision. So it happened that when the shade cloth collapsed dramatically, I was flat out on the bunk in my cabin, safely out of harm's way. Luckily, no one was hurt. I emerged for bird call, but there were few birds to call that day. I did learn that the tapered tail of Jouanin's Petrel is no longer considered diagnostic.

We spent Thursday at sea. I was on deck at 5 a.m., before sunrise at 5.15 a.m. I was paying strict attention, hoping for a Swinhoe's Storm Petrel. These all-dark storm petrels are very difficult to identify. They are medium sized with a slightly forked tail. I saw dozens of Bulwer's Petrels, more than 150 Wedge-tailed Shearwaters, one Abbott's Booby and one Masked Booby. As usual, it was hot. At morning tea time I staggered down to the dining room for a drink. No sooner had I poured myself a glass of refreshing Gaterade, than a call came from the bow: 'Swinhoe's'. I downed my drink and rushed back on deck. When I say 'rushed', I mean that I walked as quickly as I could on a moving boat. Of course, the Swinhoe's was long gone. After that I was reluctant to leave the deck and examined every dark seabird to the best of my ability. There were several contenders for classification as Swinhoe's. Eventually Rohan called one. I had a good look before I wrote it down in my notebook, grinning from ear to ear. My notes confirm that we recorded 12 Swinhoe's that day, as well as another eight birds that might have been either Swinhoe's or equally Matsudaira's (and if the experts can't tell, there's no hope for the likes of me).

That night I suffered from cramp and realized that I had not been drinking enough Gaterade. At breakfast I asked for Gaterade, but was told that they were running low and advised to take magnesium tablets. I thanked the woman for her helpful advice and politely resisted the temptation to ask where I might purchase magnesium tables in the middle of the Indian Ocean.

On Friday we were scheduled to arrive at Ashmore Reef, and before that I was hoping for a Matsudaira's Storm Petrel. These large, dark storm petrels have a pale crescent on their upperwings and a very deeply forked tail. Or so I'm told. I did not see one. When we were 14 nautical miles from Ashmore, Rohan pointed out the aqua halo. I put on my polaroid sunglasses so I could see it too. A haze shimmered over the reef proclaiming its presence to the world. Quite picturesque.

On arriving at Ashmore Reef I forgot my disappointment in not seeing Matsudaira's Storm Petrels, in my excitement at what might be lurking in the bushes, waiting for me on West Island. I was eager to go ashore. Again, it was hot. On this trip the horizon always appeared misty because of the very high humidity. There were three small boats moored nearby. I was told that they were to return asylum seekers to Indonesia. The boats people arrived in were burnt on the beach.

After lunch we went ashore on West Island, and were confronted with a major shock. It took several minutes for the ramifications of the situation to sink in. What I had considered a conservative wish list was now revealed to be totally unrealistic. Far worse, West Island may never again be a hot spot for vagrants. The island was suffering from severe drought, and probably as a result, thousands of seabirds had invaded. Most of the vegetation was dead. There was no food for passerines. Any vagrants that did fly in would not stay. None of the vines that had tripped me up on my previous visit remained. Some of the Octopus Bushes had live leaves and I hoped that it was possible they could recover. Others had been taken over by creepers and were probably condemned. One of the two Coconut Palms had fallen over.

When we landed on the beach our ears were assailed with a very loud noise, like static radio turned to maximum volume. After we clambered over the sand dunes we could see the source of the noise: thousands of nesting seabirds. The biggest colony comprised more than 25,000 Sooty Terns. There were also 900 Black Noddies, 800 Brown Noddies (previously called Common Noddies), 100 Bridled Terns, 62 Greater Crested Terns and 20 Lesser Noddies. All these birds nest on the ground. In the bushes there were Pacific Reef Herons (birds I used to call Eastern Reef Egrets) with their unbelievably ugly green featherless chicks, and about a dozen Red-footed Boobies. One booby had a few sticks placed in imitation of a nest. Rohan said this was called 'play nesting'. Some boobies were nesting seriously. They sat high in the bushes, the sun glowing through their red feet and lighting them up like Christmas lanterns. If the boobies decide to call West Island home and the colony grows, they will inevitably destroy what little vegetation remains.

There were dozens of Buff-banded Rails, enjoying the feast of seabird eggs lying on the ground ready for the taking. Hermit crabs also took advantage of this free tucker laid out before them. Each time we visited West Island (which we did on eight occasions on this trip) we walked around the island twice (5km in total). It was very disappointing to see a freshly laid egg on our first circuit, which had been destroyed by our second tour.

Every time we visited we saw just three Eurasian Tree Sparrows, a couple of Rainbow Bee-eaters, a single Eastern Yellow Wagtail, a handful of Nankeen Night Herons and up to 10 Sacred Kingfishers. You can imagine just how carefully I examined these kingfishers, looking at the shapes of their bills and the colour of their underparts, hoping to convert them into Collared Kingfishers. I did not succeed. There were hundreds of Pacific Reef Herons, predominantly white ones, but a few dark ones too. We usually saw Oriental Plovers and Horsfield's Bronze Cuckoos.

On our first visit we all had great views of an Island Monarch. I was thrilled to tick something off my wish list. By then I had grasped the fact that my wish list was no more than fanciful fiction, and to be able to cross something off it was an exceptional privilege.

As I say, we visited West Island on eight occasions. Each time I tried to remain optimistic in the oppressive heat. We certainly remained diligent, inspecting every bush assiduously. Once someone saw a Barn Swallow, and on one visit we all had lovely close views of a Black Bittern. On our sixth visit we saw the Indonesian race of the Rose-crowned Fruit Dove, which perversely does not have a rose crown. It is known as the Grey-capped Fruit Dove and is a potential future split. On that visit we also saw my third lifer for the trip, an Edible Nest Swiftlet. This bird flew, admittedly quite fast, but obligingly at eye level, and returned several times, giving everyone a good look.

Every time we visited we saw Rainbow Bee-eaters.

We also saw Nankeen Night Herons.

A few Pacific Reef Herons were dark;
most were white.

A great view of an Island Monarch.

After that excitement, on our seventh and second last visit we were jittery with expectation. Some people saw some White-headed Stilts (previously called Black-winged Stilts) but I didn't. However, everyone saw a beautiful Oriental Cuckoo that helpfully flew right over our heads. We'd been surprised at this species' absence until then. The best bird that day was the Indonesian race of the Arafura Fantail, known as the Supertramp Fantail and given species status by some authorities, though not by the IOC, the authority that I use.

Each morning we left at 5 a.m. and took the tinnies as far inshore as the tide allowed. The sky was always full of a thousand Sooty Terns, a handful of frigatebirds and one or two Red-tailed and White-tailed Tropicbirds. When a Sooty Tern flew near the boat the turquoise water reflected on the bird's white underparts, giving it the appearance of a pretty aqua tint.

As well as birds on the island we saw fire ant trails and eight dead Green Turtles. Coming ashore to lay eggs is a dangerous enterprise. We saw turtles coming ashore each day. I was told that there are Hawksbill and Loggerhead Turtles on East Island, but only Green Turtles on West Island. Each evening as we left West Island, the sun was setting and thousands of hermit crabs swarmed in a line to the sea. It was quite a spectacle – as were the sunsets. Picture the black silhouette of the single Coconut Palm against a pretty pink sky and a silver crescent moon above. Once we watched the huge red orb of the sun slowly sink over the horizon while the dark, colourless sky hung above.

There were always one or two Red-tailed Tropicbirds.

While we inspected West Island each morning and afternoon, we were free in the middle of the day for other activities. On Saturday we went to East Island and Splittgerber Cay. On Sunday we called at Middle Island and an adjacent sand bar known as the Horseshoe.

My memory of East Island is of hundreds of juvenile Lesser Frigatebirds sitting on their nests. These big babies are able to fly but choose to remain at home to be fed by their parents (sound familiar?). The Sooty Terns lay a single egg and sit above it, not on it, shading it with their wings. My notes say that there were more than 7,000 of them.

There were thousands of waders at Splittgerber Cay. Those of us with scopes had good views. I recorded 22 species, while others saw more. The most exciting birds for me were (again) seven Asian Dowitchers. The most numerous were almost a thousand Red-necked Stints, almost as many Grey-tailed Tattlers, and hundreds of Great Knots, Ruddy Turnstones, Sanderlings, Greater Sand Plovers and Curlew Sandpipers. There were more than a hundred Pacific Golden Plovers, Bar-tailed Godwits and Common Greenshanks.

At Splittgerber Cay, we saw hundreds of Grey-tailed Tattlers.

There were hundreds of Greater Sand Plovers.

Booby heaven.

On Sunday we visited Middle Island and this time we were permitted to land. I think we would have seen all the same species had we stayed in our tinnies. As we approached, Rohan saw a big white bird. There was a frisson of excitement throughout the tinnie. Whatever could it be? Rohan reached for binoculars and we all held our breath. It turned out to be a leucistic frigatebird. Later, photos revealed that it had a red eye, so we decided it was albino. The juvenile Lesser Frigatebirds were about to fledge. There were hundreds of Sooty Terns and well over a hundred Greater Crested Terns with eggs.

If East Island was noddy heaven in 2014, Middle Island was booby heaven in 2016. There were about 500 Brown Boobies, about 30 Masked Boobies and 20 Red-footed Boobies. All of the Red-footed Boobies were white-phase birds, except for one dark-phase individual with a blue face. We learnt very quickly to keep our distance from the Masked Boobies. These birds don't make a nest, but lay their two eggs on the ground and vigorously defend a small territory around the eggs, jabbing at any intruder with a vengeance. Although they lay two eggs, they usually only raise one chick.

The Horseshoe sandbank was another wader hotspot. Again, those with scopes had great views. There were thousands of birds, including hundreds of Bar-tailed Godwits, Ruddy Turnstones, Greater Sand Plovers, Grey-tailed Tattlers, Red-necked Stints, Sanderlings, Grey Plovers and Pacific Golden Plovers, as well as Pacific Reef Herons, Little Terns and Black Noddies. The sheer number of birds was overwhelming. Instead of being excited by hundreds of godwits, I found myself looking for the single Terek Sandpiper. Such is the nature of the twitcher: not happy unless every tickable species is ticked.

Of the eight birds on my supposedly conservative wish list, I saw just two: Swinhoe's Storm Petrel and the Island Monarch. The Grey-capped Fruit Dove and Supertramp Fantail were just races according to the IOC, so they didn't add to my Australian total. The only other lifer I saw was the Edible Nest Swiftlet. So, once again, I came home from Ashmore with just three ticks under my belt. Such are the fortunes of birdwatching. Had I been prepared to tolerate *Flying Fish II* in 2015, I could have seen 10 lifers.

Brown Booby with egg.

15 Chat Island

Chat Island is the only island in this book which is not offshore.
It is an inland island, indeed an artificial island, created when the
Ord River was dammed to create Lake Argyle in the 1970s.

KEY SPECIES

- Oriental Plover
- Little Curlew
- Long-toed Stint
- Ruff (female is called Reeve)
- White-quilled Rock Pigeon
- Yellow Chat
- Sandstone Shrikethrush
- Horsfield's Bush Lark

Right: Flooding the lake marooned Short-eared Rock Wallabies.

Lake Argyle is the largest man-made lake in the southern hemisphere, and it provides both irrigation and hydroelectricity. In flood the lake can cover a massive 2,000km². The making of Lake Argyle has created many islands, some of which are home to endearing marooned Short-eared Rock Wallabies. These islands have no official names, but the one I visited when I was last there in 2009 is nicknamed 'Chat Island' by the man who runs boat tours on the lake, because (he says) there are so many Yellow Chats present. I hoped this was more than tourist hype. It was Yellow Chats that had lured me to Chat Island.

I was part of a small group of birders on a Black Grasswren tour run by Kirrama Tours (this company is no longer operational). We started in Darwin, visited Kakadu, then went on to Kununurra, from whence we flew to the Mitchell Plateau for the grasswrens. It was also from Kununurra that we visited Lake Argyle. The tour brochure promised: 'One day we leave very early in the morning and do a birdwatching cruise on Lake Argyle, and highlights are Yellow Chats, White-quilled Rock Pigeons, Sandstone Shrikethrushes and possibly Purple-crowned Fairywrens plus a lot of water birds.' We did not see Purple-crowned Fairywrens, but otherwise the brochure was accurate. There were lots of White-quilled Rock Pigeons and Sandstone Shrikethrushes.

I don't remember much about the little boat that ferried us around Lake Argyle. I do remember that I didn't like getting on and off as the steps on the ladder were razor sharp on bare feet.

We'd certainly seen 'a lot of water birds' by the time we reached Chat Island. I remember darters, cormorants, pelicans, Magpie Geese, Black-necked Storks and Glossy Ibis. There were Brolgas and jacanas, whistling ducks, White-headed Stilts, dotterels and lapwings, Pied Herons and egrets. Just for good measure there were Sacred Kingfishers too. My notebook records 31 species before we reached Chat Island.

The first bird I saw on Chat Island was an Australian Bustard, then Australian Pratincoles and Magpie-larks. A Red-capped Plover ran along the shoreline, running then pausing, then running some more. I'm not sure how large the island is – a few hectares at most. I don't remember any trees. I sat on the boat and contemplated my options. Birding was quite good from the boat. Did I really want to get off? This would involve taking off my shoes and socks, clambering off the boat into ankle-deep water, wading ashore, finding somewhere to sit down to dry my feet and put my shoes on, then standing up again without anything to hold on to – all of this without making a spectacle of myself. Before I'd come to a decision, we saw chats from the

There were lots of White-quilled Rock Pigeons.

And many Sandstone Shrikethrushes.

We saw Magpie Geese.

White-headed Stilt.

boat – a female first, then a gaudy yellow male. I smiled. Mission accomplished. Now there was no need to get off the boat. A sea eagle flew overhead, confirming that birding from the boat was pretty good. The Yellow Chats were playing on the island, inviting me ashore.

My fellow passengers were incredulous that I'd even consider not joining them on the island. In the end, peer pressure won out over the discomfort of a wet walk. I put my shoes in my backpack and climbed down the knife-edged ladder. The water weeds were slimy between my toes. I painted a smile on my face and thought about the birdy pleasures that lay ahead.

As it happened, I'd added Common Greenshanks, Whiskered Terns, Far Eastern Curlews and Sharp-tailed Sandpipers to my bird list before my shoelaces were tied. It was the Long-toed Stint that confirmed to me that my decision to go ashore was the right one. When I added a Reeve and a Little Curlew to my list, I began to feel smug. I'd have seen the Green Pygmy Geese and the Nankeen Night Herons from the boat, and perhaps the Hardheads and the Australasian Grebes, but I would not have seen

A Red-capped Plover ran, paused, then ran some more.

A gaudy male Yellow Chat.

I saw female Yellow Chats from the boat.

the Rainbow Bee-eaters, or the Wood or Marsh Sandpipers. I certainly wouldn't have seen Horsfield's Bush Lark or the Oriental Plover, or the Buff-banded Rail. On the other hand, I probably would have seen the Gull-billed Tern and Pallid Cuckoo.

On our return trip we added the Eastern Osprey and Red-winged Parrots to the bird list. We all had silly grins on our faces.

What a phenomenal little island. I'm not sure how many Yellow Chats there were – perhaps a dozen. The boat operator certainly employed an apt name – no tourist hype at all, but just a legitimate, appropriate, honest name.

I would not have seen Rainbow Bee-eaters from the boat.

I added Sharp-tailed Sandpipers to my bird list before my shoelaces were tied.

The Long-toed Stint endorsed my decision to go ashore.

16 Boigu Island

*I've been to Boigu Island three times: once in January 2006,
when I spent a sticky couple of hours there (and ticked my 650th
Australian bird); once in March 2016, when I spent two days there
with Richard Baxter's Birding Tours Australia; and most recently
in March 2018, again with Richard Baxter, when we simply got
wet without seeing anything new.*

KEY SPECIES

- Orange-fronted Fruit Dove
- Coroneted Fruit Dove
- Collared Imperial Pigeon
- Chestnut-breasted Cuckoo
- Uniform Swiftlet
- Papuan Spine-tailed Swift
- House Swift
- Coconut Lorikeet
- Mimic Honeyeater

- Singing Starling
- Red-capped Flowerpecker
- **Local races of:**
- Orange-footed Scrubfowl
- Eclectus Parrot
- Red-headed Myzomela
- Tawny-breasted Honeyeater
- Willie Wagtail
- Leaden Flycatcher

BOIGU ISLAND ★

AUSTRALIA

Right: Boigu is Australia's most northerly inhabited island.

There were two reasons for my return to the island in 2018. First, on my second visit I achieved one very exciting lifer: a Coroneted Fruit Dove, a new bird for the Australian list (sadly, this record was not accepted by BARC, the Birds Australia Rarities Committee, which doesn't mean that we didn't see it, just that our photos weren't good enough to persuade the experts). I reckoned anywhere I'd seen such a rare bird was worth a return visit. Who knows, I might be lucky again. The second reason for my return visit was to see a Coconut Lorikeet. I thought I'd been unlucky not to see this relatively common bird on my previous trips and dearly wanted to add it to my list.

Boigu is Australia's most northerly inhabited island, situated in Torres Strait just 6km from Papua New Guinea (PNG). The island is 18km long and comprises 89.6km². The population is something under 300 people. Most of the island is subject to flooding and the interior is mainly swamp, while the coast is mangroves and mudflats. The island was formed by sediments flowing down rivers in PNG and being deposited in the Torres Strait.

In January 2006, Roger and I were attending a Bamega Bird Week run by Kirrama Tours. Bamega is on the northern tip of Cape York. An optional extra was a flight to Boigu Island in a small plane. This sounded very exciting and I was eager to go. Several keen birders put their hands up, so there would be two trips. Rog and I were in the second group. The first plane-load went on Sunday, and when the people returned I was naturally very keen to hear about what they'd seen. I soon learnt that there was an unidentified Asian myna near the public toilets – a bird never seen in Australia before. I was told that I must take my camera and get a shot of this exciting new bird. My 300mm lens was genuinely heavy and always seemed heavier in the

sweaty heat of the tropics, but I took it with me to Boigu in the hope of finding this tantalizing 'toilet bird'.

On Monday morning we left Bamega at 5.30 a.m., arriving on Boigu at 7.15 a.m. As we climbed out of the plane we were walloped with a wall of fiery hot air. I thought it had been hot at Bamega, but Boigu was unbelievably hotter. We were in charge; we had hired the plane. We could stay as long as we liked and we were all keen birders. We'd paid for the privilege of visiting Boigu and each one of us wanted to see every bird there was to see – and I particularly wanted to see the mystery myna, yesterday's so-called 'toilet bird'. Our leader (Lloyd Nielsen) made himself known to the village chief and we were free to wander around the township. I made straight for the toilets. Naturally, there were no birds in sight.

I remember a friendly Willie Wagtail (race *melaleuca*), and a pair of Leaden Flycatchers (race *papuana*), together with a pair of Shining Flycatchers playing close by in a low bush, and of course I remember the Collared Imperial Pigeon that flew low overhead. This was my 650th Australian bird. Apart from that, I remember the heat. You will understand how unpleasant the heat was when I say that we all agreed to leave the island before 11 a.m. We were all keen birders. This was exciting new territory and we'd paid dearly for the privilege of being here. Yet we chose to leave. Who knows what wonderful avian treats we were denying ourselves? But we had no option really. The heat was simply overwhelming. Like the motion of a boat at sea, it was inescapable, ever present. It sucked the life out of us. I took a photo of PNG. It seemed so close that you could reach out and touch it.

Torresian Imperial Pigeons commute daily from Papua New Guinea to Boigu.

Yesterday's group had seen 47 birds. Our group saw the same – although personally I only managed 39, and 18 of these were waders and waterbirds. We saw several honeyeaters and I noted that the male Varied Triller had no buff on his undertail. The Collared Imperial Pigeon was the only new bird I saw. All the rest were old familiar friends (although I don't see Chestnut-breasted Cuckoos every day). The Common Cicadabird is a different race from the one I'd seen in Cairns, and the Torresian Imperial Pigeons we called TIPs were quite common, commuting daily from PNG to Boigu. These birds were formerly called Pied Imperial Pigeons, or PIPs, which somehow sounds a whole lot nicer than TIPs. There's another bird called a Pied Imperial Pigeon in the New Guinea field guides, so it makes sense to find another name for our Australian bird.

I did not see the tantalizing 'toilet bird', the unidentified Asian myna, and sadly I did not see any lost PNG rarities that had managed to stray a little too far south in order to get on to my life list. Of course I was delighted to achieve the 650 milestone, but I came home thinking of just one word in association with Boigu: hot.

My second trip to Boigu was completely and utterly different, at least in so far as the preparation went. We didn't just hop on a plane for a morning's outing. I was with Richard Baxter in a boat called the *Eclipse*, and not counting the crew there were 10 of us. Richard had led a group to the same places the week before, so we benefited from all their findings. I flew to Cairns, then to Horn Island off the tip of Cape York, where we boarded the *Eclipse*.

A great deal of preparation was required for this trip. No one had mentioned crocodiles on our first visit. Now we were instructed to beware, not only of crocodiles, but of extremely venomous and aggressive snakes: the Papuan Taipan and the Papuan Black Snake. Gaiters were a non-negotiable essential item of clothing. The gaiters were uncomfortable and difficult to put on. I suspected they were unnecessary but they did focus the mind and keep us aware that we were in a foreign inhospitable environment. When we arrived on Horn Island we were told a rumour about a local on Boigu who'd been bitten by a snake the previous week. He'd been flown to Cairns and had his leg amputated. Whether or not the story was true, it succeeded in making me persevere with my onerous gaiters. We were told that last week's group had seen four snakes, but I did not believe this. As it turned out we didn't see any snakes, or – much to some people's disappointment – any crocodiles either.

Furthermore, there was the danger of several potentially lethal mosquito-borne diseases, including, but not restricted to, malaria and Japanese encephalitis. I bought anti-malarial tablets (which I was instructed to start taking a week before I left home), and was horrified to learn that one of the potential side effects was diarrhoea. I couldn't imagine suffering from diarrhoea on a tiny boat with only two toilets and 12 other people to share them with. As it happened, I took my anti-malaria pills and suffered no side effects at all. As to the encephalitis, I had to talk hard to persuade my doctor to immunise me. She'd never been to the Torres Strait, but she had access to a website that informed her the disease was no longer prevalent. I trusted Richard. If he said we should be vaccinated, I wanted to be vaccinated. Of course my doctor finally agreed, but she made me sit in the waiting room afterwards so she could deal with the pernicious side effects I would inevitably endure. I suffered no side effects and after 20 minutes she let me go home. In the past, to protect against encephalitis, people had three injections a month apart. Now a single vaccination lasts a decade, so I was already prepared for future trips to the Torres Strait.

Another precaution against mosquitoes involved soaking all our clothes in permethrin. This I dutifully did (although I forgot to soak my hat). It was quite a performance. I remember having trouble finding enough shady spots in which to hang all my shirts and trousers. Luckily, today you can purchase clothes already treated with insect repellent, and it works.

I hoped that all this assiduous preparation would result in many more new birds – but it did not. We'd flown to Horn Island, then boarded the *Eclipse*. Sometimes Richard's groups visit Saibai first, sometimes it's Boigu. It depends on the tides. In 2016 we spent the first three days on Saibai. Early on Thursday morning (two o'clock to be precise) we left Saibai, arriving at Boigu just before 7 a.m. I sat in the galley enjoying a cup of coffee while swifts and swallows swooped around the boat. We identified House Swifts and Uniform Swiftlets. Of course I was hoping for Papuan Spine-tailed Swifts, but they stubbornly refused to put in an appearance.

After breakfast we went ashore. I carried as little as possible. The first drama was the horrible metal ladder we had to climb up to get on to the jetty – the razor-sharp steel rungs were designed to inflict maximum pain to my city slicker's tender bare feet. The second drama was filling out forms at the municipal offices for permission to be on the island. This was only a drama because I'd left my glasses on the boat: I was prepared for birdwatching not bureaucracy. The township was neat and tidy, with lawns mown and not a trace of litter anywhere – quite a contrast to Saibai. Signs reminded residents not to leave water lying about where mosquitoes might breed. Other signs asserted that trading in Dugongs was illegal. The local indigenous people were permitted to hunt for their own use only. Singing Starlings were common around the town, and they would have been a lifer for me if I hadn't seen them a couple of days before on Saibai.

Our first stop was the tip, probably the best spot for birding on Boigu. This is very close to the sea, and muddy and slippery, but held the expectation of something Very Good about to happen. It was hot, but nothing like the unbearable conditions of January 2006. This was March – that could explain the difference. It was still hot, but tolerable. Last week's group had seen an Orange-fronted Fruit Dove at this spot – a new bird for Australia. We were keen to see it too. We improvised seating arrangements: someone found an old filing cabinet, some used upturned buckets, others found fallen trees. Eventually I found a most uncomfortable unstable three-legged plastic chair. We sat and we waited. I remember a very long, very hot, uneventful wait.

We saw White-breasted Woodswallows, an Oriental Dollarbird, a Whistling Kite, a Common Cicadabird and lots of Pied Herons. A couple of photographers among us got bored and wandered off, wanting to photograph a Red-capped Flowerpecker.

We sat comfortably as we waited for our rare fruit dove.

We saw an Oriental Dollarbird.

Whistling Kite.

All of a sudden, without any warning, the tide turned and water gushed at us from all directions. I was nearly marooned but managed to escape. The photographers were caught and had to wade out in waist-deep water. We left at 11.30 a.m. and walked to the jetty. As soon as we arrived it was apparent that the sea was too rough for us to board Zodiacs, so we went birding instead. We saw waders (Whimbrels, sandpipers, tattlers, stints, sand plovers and lapwings). We walked along a levy bank with water on both sides of us. Richard showed us where he'd once seen a cinnamon morph of a Black Bittern, but there were no bitterns there on this day. In the afternoons we took the Zodiacs up the river – one river that day and another river the next. We saw crabs of various colours and several golden orb spiders, but very few birds. I remember Whimbrels and Shining Flycatchers.

We took the Zodiacs up a river.

There were few birds but there were always Whimbrels.

The next morning (Friday) saw us back at the tip before dawn. This was when we saw our Coroneted Fruit Dove, a very exciting bird – new for the Australian list. It was exciting, but I'm sorry I can't say we all had good views. The bird flew overhead, a dark silhouette that Richard identified later from photographs. We also saw a Collared Imperial Pigeon – just one bird in flight, and that was the only one we saw for the trip. I had thought these birds would be common after my previous visit.

On this day, instead of a tidal surge the water came as rain in the form of serious monsoonal downpours. We sheltered under the verandah of the municipal offices. We did manage to check out the town water-supply dam for waders, before returning to the *Eclipse*. On Saturday we returned to Horn Island. It was a rough trip.

My third trip to Boigu in March 2018 was a bit of an anticlimax. Most of us had been there before and knew what to expect. This time we came armed with folding stools so we sat comfortably while we waited for our rare fruit dove – which never appeared. I had a walking stick with a fold-down seat, and although it was made with a taller person in mind it worked quite well. The long, hot, uneventful wait of my memory was, on this occasion, transformed into a not quite so hot, fascinating cavalcade of birds. There were White-breasted Woodswallows, Olive-backed Sunbirds, Rainbow Bee-eaters, Willie Wagtails, Torresian Crows and lots of Oriental Dollarbirds. There were Common Cicadabirds, Superb Fruit Doves and Orange-footed Scrubfowl (race *duperyii*). Meanwhile, flying overhead there were Channel-billed Cuckoos, White-bellied Sea Eagles, TIPs and one New Guinea Eclectus Parrot (race *polychlocos*). There were Spangled Drongos, Collared Imperial Pigeons and Large-billed Gerygones. We watched a large flock of starlings fly above us and debated whether they were Metallic or Singing Starlings. Metallic Starlings have long, tapered tails, whereas the tails of their Singing cousins are short and square. Some of us saw long tails; others saw short, square tails. We finally realized that this was a mixed flock of both species. I wonder if this experience felt not quite so hot as my memory of the previous occasion because I was constantly entertained by a wonderful array of exciting birds. We left at 9.30 a.m. and my notebook recorded 42 species.

The week before we visited Boigu, Richard had taken another group of birders to a spot a little beyond the tip to see Red-capped Flowerpeckers. They'd seen not only flowerpeckers, but also a Mimic Honeyeater, a New Guinea species not on the Australian list. You can imagine how much we wanted that bird.

If you go to Boigu you'll find the Coroneted Fruit Dove site just beyond the tip. Just beyond that, up an unbelievably muddy track, is a creek you can wade across. As far as I know, no crocodile has been seen here. Not far beyond the creek is a clearing, a good spot in which to look for Red-capped Flowerpeckers. About another 20m further on is another clearing, and this is where the Mimic Honeyeater was seen, or so Richard tells me – I cannot vouch for this myself. The only honeyeaters I remember in the immediate vicinity were the Tawny-breasted Honeyeater (race *saturatior*) and Red-headed Myzomela (race *infuscata*). More memorable was a bright green Emerald Monitor.

On our final morning on Boigu we started the day at the back of the airport. Here we had open skies giving excellent views of whatever chose to fly over. Not much did, apart from a Striated Heron, Nankeen Night Heron, Great Frigatebird and the ubiquitous Channel-billed Cuckoo. On the ground we saw scrubfowl and Pheasant Coucals. Sunbirds and Rufous-banded Honeyeaters were our constant companions. The most memorable occurrence that morning was a couple of planes landing, passing very low above our heads.

We visited the north of the island, hoping for Coconut Lorikeets, my main quarry for the trip. There were deer tracks in the sand. Apparently the deer swam to Boigu from New Guinea. There were some pretty weeds, but I did not see or hear any lorikeets. Sadly, without any new birds, we set off for Saibai, four hours away.

If I'm asked to sum up Boigu in one word, I'll say 'hot'. All three times when I've been there it was always uncomfortably hot. I'll probably never go there again, but if I do you'll find me beyond the tip, sitting, waiting for rare fruit doves.

Richard is the only person who can persaude me to wade through mud.

17 Saibai Island

I've visited Saibai Island twice, both times with Richard Baxter's Birding Tours Australia. The first time was in March 2016, then, most recently, in March 2018. In 2016, I saw a remarkable six lifers: two of which I expected – the Red-capped Flowerpecker and Singing Starling; two I hoped for – the Uniform Swiftlet and Gurney's Eagle; and two quite off my radar – the Pacific Swallow and Zoë's Imperial Pigeon.

KEY SPECIES

SAIBAI ISLAND ★

AUSTRALIA

- Spotted Whistling Duck
- Garganey
- Gurney's Eagle
- Pink-spotted Fruit Dove
- Collared Imperial Pigeon
- Zoë's Imperial Pigeon
- Uniform Swiftlet
- Papuan Spine-tailed Swift
- Pacific Swift
- Coconut Lorikeet
- Red-flanked Lorikeet
- Singing Starling
- Red-capped Flowerpecker

Local races of:
- Tawny-breasted Honeyeater
- Torresian Crow

Right: We had a pleasant Zodiac trip up a river.

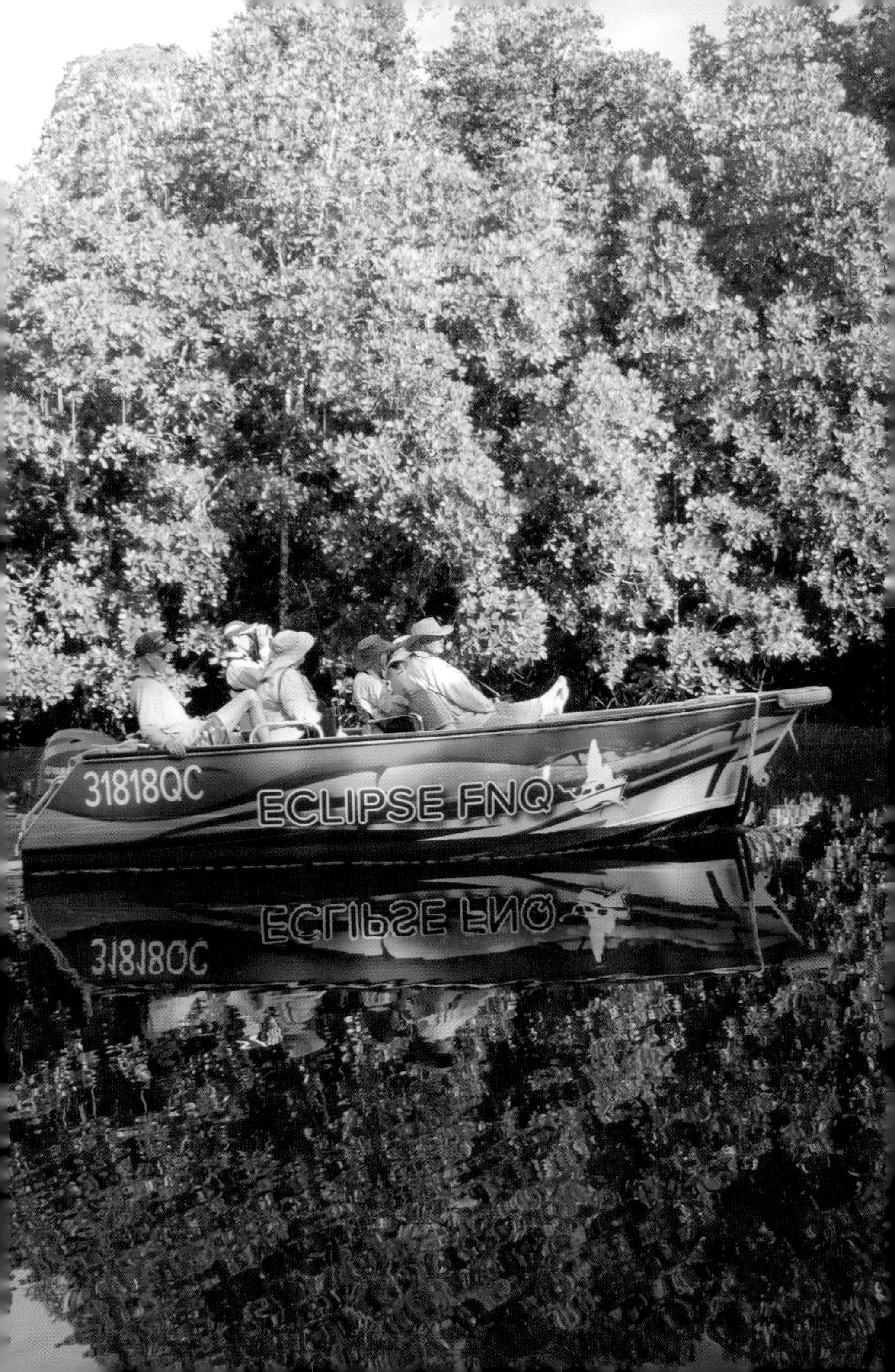
31818QC
ECLIPSE FNQ

Zoë's Imperial Pigeon had not been recorded in Australia before. In 2018, I managed two more birds: the Coconut Lorikeet (a bird I'd been disappointed to miss in 2016 and the main reason for my return to the Torres Strait two years later), and the Red-flanked Lorikeet, an unexpected rarity.

Saibai Island is 8km south of Papua New Guinea. It is about 22km long and 5km wide. The whole island is prone to flooding and comprises mainly mangrove swamps. It's all pretty flat, the highest point being 1.7m above sea level, and 2m of rain falls in every wet season. In 2016 I reckon at least half of that fell on me on the two days I spent on the island. In 2018 we were drenched several times, invariably when we were cruising in the tenders.

There are two villages on the island but we only visited one – the village of Saibai, with a population of 170 people. There is litter everywhere. One of us saw a woman come out of her front door with a plastic bag full of rubbish, then walk past a rubbish bin to dump the bag into the swamp. English is not the native tongue of the population. I'm told their language is Kalaw Kawaw Ya. Some people made us feel welcome; some did not. The children were delightfully happy. They greeted us and said 'goodbye', then giggled uncontrollably at this hilarious joke. We thought they were telling us to go home. New Guinea natives came to the island while we were there and set up a market of handicrafts. Only later did I consider that it was for our benefit. I looked at the goods on display and was not tempted to reach for my purse. Others bought crafts – woven bags, carved birds, crocodiles and dugongs. I saw a very nice carved wooden heron, but couldn't think of anyone to give it to.

The New Guinea natives set up a market of handicrafts.

Both times I visited Saibai I travelled on the fishing charter *Eclipse*. Both times we also visited Boigu and left from Horn Island. I flew to Horn Island from Cairns. Here I met Richard and the group I was to spend the next few days with, as well as last week's group that had just returned from Boigu and Saibai.

In 2016 the first bit of bad news was that no one had seen a Coconut Lorikeet. I'd thought this was going to be easy. My notes record: 'It seems *nothing* is going to be easy.' Just to rub it in, lorikeets were common on Horn Island, but they were all ordinary Rainbow Lorikeets (albeit a different race from the Victorian birds – here they were *septentrionalis*). Last week's group had good news about the presence of Garganey – a bird I'd always wanted to see, but which hadn't been seen in Australia since the avian flu of 2008. I had feared that this was a bird I'd never see and was delighted to learn that at least one Garganey was on Saibai. Even if I didn't see this particular bird on this occasion, it meant that the birds were back and there'd be other opportunities.

On Sunday we set off in the *Eclipse*. The tides decided that we'd visit Saibai first. On the way we stopped at Little Tuesday Island, so anyone who needed the Ashy-bellied White-eye for their list could go ashore. However, the tides were not in our favour. The water was too deep for wading and too shallow to allow the Zodiacs to get close to shore, so the second boat-load was restricted to four people and I remained on the *Eclipse*.

We had one interesting sighting that day of travelling. We saw a flock of 19 Rainbow Bee-eaters migrating back to PNG. I had always believed that Australia's southern Rainbow Bee-eaters migrated north in winter, but that northern birds were resident all year. I consulted HANZAB. I learnt that bee-eaters' movements are not well understood, and the birds are present in New Guinea from mid-March to mid-October. We saw birds migrating on 13 March, so that sounds about right.

It rained overnight, so when we went ashore on Saibai on Monday morning, everything was wet, muddy and slippery. As we clambered off the Zodiac, a couple of people saw lorikeets flying along the treeline. These were my much-desired Coconut Lorikeets, but I was busy getting out of the Zodiac and on to the jetty, looking at my feet not the treeline. As it turned out, I'd just missed my only opportunity of seeing Coconut Lorikeets for the week. Their presence is unpredictable. In some years they are abundant, but in 2016 they were not. As we stood on the jetty we saw some crows perched on a tower. These were the Torres Strait race of Torresian Crow (*orru*), a new race for me.

It rained again, heavily, as we looked for flowerpeckers in the cemetery. My notebook was wet through and never recovered. Nor did my shoes. The mossies were prolific and my pre-trip promethrin soaking was certainly worth the effort. We saw starlings, which we hoped might be Singing Starlings, but their long tails revealed them to be Metallic Starlings. One expanse of water that Richard said hadn't been there the previous week attracted our attention. There were swallows swooping above it; Richard said that the only swallows here would be Pacific Swallows, so we suddenly all took them seriously. Yes, Pacific Swallows they were. A very nice start to my Saibai lifers.

In the afternoon we visited the swamp where the Garganey had been seen just a few days before. Walking through ankle-deep water wearing gaiters is not something I'd do for fun. The water had risen significantly, and ducks previously with no option except the far recess of the swamp now had plenty of choice. The Garganey's choice had been to leave. There were lots of Raja Shelducks and one Black Bittern. As we stood with wet feet mourning the loss of our Garganey, a Peregrine flew over, chasing a pigeon. The photographers present did their stuff, and from their photos Richard identified the bird being chased as a Zoë's Imperial Pigeon.

On Tuesday morning we had a very pleasant Zodiac trip up a river. Mossies were in biblical proportions. We were told that the locals go crabbing up this river, but not at this time of year because there are too many mosquitoes. There were Whimbrels,

We started with a visit to Saibai's cemetery.

There were lots of Raja Shelducks.   *Bar-shouldered Doves were very common.*

Torresian Kingfishers and Shining Flycatchers. We saw a Mangrove Monitor and a pair of Whistling Kites. Bar-shouldered Doves were very common everywhere on Saibai.

In the afternoon we went back to Saibai. We chatted to a man outside the supermarket who'd been to 'the mainland' (meaning New Guinea) and caught a bird-of-paradise. He said he wanted to sell it but became very coy when we tried to negotiate with him. All he'd say was that he wanted 'a lotta money', then he'd say no more.

We saw a fruit dove, and after a fair bit of trouble identified it as Superb. Of course we were all hoping for something much rarer. Everywhere we walked there was rubbish lying on the ground. We saw Tawny-breasted Honeyeaters (race *saturatior*), different from those on Cape York. Richard led us to a clearing and showed us a male Red-capped Flowerpecker. The bird sat, posing for us, just above our heads – a very handsome bird, with a song that was quite similar to the Australian Mistletoebird's song.

Then it was back to the Garganey swamp. There was water lying everywhere, encouraging the birds to disperse. What had been hundreds of Raja Shelducks had become dozens. Richard divided us into pairs and put us in strategic spots. Nowhere was ideal. Everyone was standing in water. Cleverly I found a slight mound of dry ground and was pleased to get my feet out of the swamp. However, within a couple of minutes I was covered in Green Ants, which sent me back into the water lickety-split. Not much was happening on the swamp. I was confident that the Garganey would not return. A storm was brewing so we looked around for swifts. Almost immediately we saw Pacific Swifts (formerly known as Fork-tailed Swifts) and with them some smaller birds, which we identified as Uniform Swiftlets, a bird I'd been hoping to see.

On Wednesday morning we returned to the tip, which, we soon discovered, was too muddy to explore. With each step our feet were sucked down into the ooze. So we went back to the cemetery, where, this time, we did see Singing Starlings. Some observant people saw Red-flanked Lorikeets, but I did not. I watched dragonflies eating mosquitoes, catching them cleverly in mid-air.

At noon we returned to the jetty and boarded the Zodiac to return to the *Eclipse* for lunch. A large raptor flew overhead and we all had great views of a Gurney's Eagle. Richard said that this was the fifth record for Australia. I left Saibai delighted with my six lifers, but disappointed that I hadn't seen Coconut Lorikeets. I'd also been hoping for Spotted Whistling Ducks and Papuan Spine-tailed Swifts. There was nothing for it – I had to go back again.

I'd booked my next trip (March 2018) before I disembarked from the *Eclipse*, so the mud, heat and mossies can't have been that bad. However, in the intervening two years, whenever I thought of returning to Saibai it was the mud, heat and mossies I remembered first, before my remarkable six lifers. That says it all.

Before I left home in March 2018, I knew that Richard's first group of birders in the Torres Strait had had some good sightings. As well as the expected flowerpecker and starlings, they'd seen a Pink-spotted Fruit Dove and (even better from my point of view) Coconut Lorikeets. This first group of birders was already back home and the second group was preparing to leave, when the third group (including me) arrived at Horn Island. The second group had not had much luck. Not only had they dipped on the Mimic Honeyeater on Boigu, but they hadn't seen the Pink-spotted Fruit Dove on Saibai and, worse, they hadn't heard or seen any lorikeets anywhere.

I joined Richard's third group because it was the only one scheduled to visit a third island, Ugar. All Richard's Torres Strait trips visited Boigu and Saibai. I hoped that going to another island, not well known to birders, might reveal something special. As it turned out, Cyclone Nora decided that we were not to visit Ugar at all so I'll probably never know what birding delights were denied me.

In 2018 we began our first trip to Saibai with a visit to the familiar cemetery. This time there were no mossies. My notebook records 27 species in the little over two hours we were there. There were swifts, swiftlets, starlings, fantails, flycatchers, and Torresian and Collared Imperial Pigeons, but, sadly, no Pink-spotted Fruit Doves. We visited the cemetery on two other occasions and the most exciting sighting was hundreds of Pacific Swifts. I reckoned we'd seen a thousand by 7 a.m. And still they came. They'd petered out by 7.30 a.m., leaving us all drained with the thrill of it.

We looked for lorikeets in the township on Saibai, then inspected the sewerage farm. A local told us of parrots near a beach on the south-west side of the island. We inspected this location with no luck.

Because of the cyclone *Eclipse* was moored in the channel between Saibai and Kaumag. This was where we'd seen the Gurney's Eagle in 2016. We saw it again here in 2018. In fact we saw three, but I only had distant views this time, nothing like the wonderful close-up inspection we'd had two years before.

Some lorikeets flew over the boat. I was on the top deck with Jenny Spry (Australia's top female birder), and we were the only two of the group lucky enough to see them. They screeched as they flew, as lorikeets do. I saw just black silhouettes, but Jenny (bless her) saw yellow and red. 'They were not Coconuts!' she proclaimed, and I confess I was momentarily disappointed. I'd come all this way to see Coconut Lorikeets. I'd seen nothing new on Boigu. We were denied access to Ugar and now, when I'd finally seen my lorikeets, I was being told I could not add the Coconut Lorikeet to my life list. My disappointment was short-lived. Our birds were quickly identified as Red-flanked Lorikeets, much rarer than their Coconut cousins.

What's more, the next morning I stayed on *Eclipse*, watching for lorikeets, while others enjoyed a river cruise in the tenders. I was rewarded with dozens of Coconut Lorikeets flying by. They were in small flocks of four to eight birds, flying at different heights, some showing colour, some high ones just silhouettes. One pair landed in a nearby mangrove, so I saw them perched too. I came home happy. Cyclone Nora might have stopped me from visiting Ugar, but if we hadn't sheltered in that channel I probably wouldn't have seen either species of lorikeet.

The Red-capped Flowerpecker posed for us, just above our heads.

We sheltered between Saibai and Kaumag.

18 Raine Island

I went to Raine Island for one reason only: to see a Herald Petrel. Raine Island is the only place in Australia where Herald Petrels are known to breed (suggestions in the 1980s that they bred on North Keeling Island have never been confirmed).

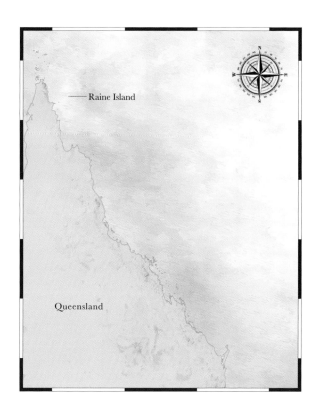

Raine Island

Queensland

RAINE ISLAND

AUSTRALIA

Right: Raine Island is the only known place in Australia where Herald Petrels nest.

I did see a Herald Petrel, so you'd think the trip was 100 per cent successful. Yet, every time I think of Raine Island, I remember the Leach's Storm Petrel that I'm sure I saw, but didn't feel I could count because nobody else saw it. Such is human nature. Why don't I celebrate my successes instead of lamenting my failures? Truth be told, I really only glimpsed it. Leach's Storm Petrels can have either a white rump or a dark rump. This bird was dark rumped. All I saw was a small dark bird with a forked tail. It looked like a Welcome Swallow. Add it to my list of Might Have Beens.

Along with Browse Island and Cabbage Tree Island, Raine is one of three islands in this book that I have not set foot upon (see page 7), but I have sailed around it.

Raine Island is a 32ha coral cay on the outer edge of the Great Barrier Reef, some 620km north-north-west of Cairns and 120km east-north-east of Cape Grenville. It is shaped like a raindrop, hence the name (don't ask me where the 'e' came from). Raine Island is part of the Great Barrier Reef Marine Park and public access to it is denied. It is most famous for having the world's largest breeding population of Green Turtles, but it is also the most significant tropical seabird breeding site in the Great Barrier Reef. Queensland legislation established the Raine Island Corporation 'to promote research into and to ensure preservation and protection of natural and cultural heritage resources of Raine Island'. The island was mined for guano in the 1890s. The seas here are treacherous – there were more than 30 shipwrecks in the vicinity. As a result, in 1844, on orders from the British Admiralty, a beacon was built on the island, using convict labour and local materials. This is the oldest European structure in the Australian tropics.

BirdLife Australia has declared Raine Island to be a Key Biodiversity Area (KBA). KBAs are priority places for bird conservation. Raine Island accommodates more than 1 per cent of the world's population of nesting Masked and Brown Boobies, and Brown and Black Noddies. In addition, populations of Herald Petrels, Red-footed Boobies and Red-tailed Tropicbirds are regionally significant.

Personally, I'm of the view that the fact that Raine Island is the only known place in Australia where Herald Petrels nest is of most significance. Herald Petrels are classified as Vulnerable. Red-tailed Tropicbirds are classified as Near Threatened. None of the other birds mentioned has a conservation classification.

Herald Petrels breed in winter in burrows, but note this: there are fewer than five pairs nesting on Raine Island. The reason why these birds don't attract a higher classification than Vulnerable is that they are genetically the same population as the birds breeding on Round Island in Mauritius. A female banded while breeding on Raine Island in 1984 was recaptured breeding on Round Island in 2006.

Raine Island has more than 1 per cent of the world population of Masked Boobies.

The island also has more than 1 per cent of the world population of Brown Boobies.

Richard Baxter's Birding Tours Australia ran three consecutive trips from Lockhart River to Raine Island in September 2015, on the boat *Eclipse*. Each trip took nine or 10 eager twitchers and everyone saw a Herald Petrel. I was on the third trip, which turned out to be the best for calm seas and pleasant weather. I also had the best cabin on the boat: it was a double on the same level as the galley and the bathrooms. Everyone else was accommodated below. My trip left Lockhart River on Friday, 18 September and returned on Tuesday, 22 September. Through no fault of my own, I was an hour late arriving in Lockhart River, holding everyone up. The plane from Cairns to Lockhart River ignored the schedule and flew to Coen instead, but as no one had been informed of this revised timetable, we waited an hour in the hot sun for a passenger who didn't turn up. There are no air-conditioned terminals at Coen airport. When we finally arrived at Lockhart River, there were my eight fellow passengers waiting impatiently for me, plus last week's 10 passengers, waiting to fly out on the plane I'd just arrived in. So we set sail on Friday, very optimistically, knowing that both previous trips had seen the petrel. We saw our quarry at 3.20 p.m. on Saturday, where the water was 600m deep.

Very little is known about Herald Petrels. We don't know what they eat, except for the fact that their diet includes cephalopods. We don't know how they feed, or know where they go when they're not breeding. We do know that they like deep water. According to Onley and Scofield, Herald Petrels are 'polymorphic, occurring in light, intermediate and dark phases'. They are described as a 'medium sized slim, long- and narrow-winged petrel of the Pacific with relatively long tail, usually held tightly closed in flight and appearing quite pointed'. Our bird very cooperatively sat on the water beside the boat, giving us all excellent views.

We travelled a total of 315 nautical miles on the *Eclipse* and the deepest water we traversed was an impressive 3km deep. On the return trip Richard took people ashore at Sunday Island looking for Ashy-bellied White-eyes. I stayed on board. I'd seen these birds before, and the island looked quite rugged.

You might think Raine Island is a long way to go to see one new species, but those of us who'd looked at the blank space beside Herald Petrel on our bird list for decades were only too pleased to jump at the chance to fill that blank space with a place and a date. Thank you once again, Richard Baxter.

The population of Red-footed Boobies is regionally significant.

19 Bedarra Island

It's been many years since I've visited Bedarra. I remember a tropical paradise with secluded beaches and waving palm trees. I recall sipping champagne on the patio at sunset while a Large-tailed Nightjar rehearsed his chop chop chop *call from a nearby palm tree. Again and again and again, with unrelenting monotony.*

KEY SPECIES

- Pacific Baza
- Brahminy Kite
- Rose-crowned Fruit Dove
- Large-tailed Nightjar
- Australian Swiftlet
- Noisy Pitta
- Varied Triller
- Spectacled Monarch
- Tawny Grassbird
- Olive-backed Sunbird

Right: Every night a Large-tailed Nightjar called monotonously.

Bedarra is where I saw my first Olive-backed Sunbird's nests and encountered my first Noisy Pittas. Of course I fell in love with them. They were so very friendly running around on the rainforest floor, a vibrant splash of tropical colour.

Bedarra is one of Queensland's Family Group of islands, situated about halfway between Townsville and Cairns. There are 16 islands in the family: Dunk is the father, Bedarra the mother and there are 14 children. Bedarra is triangular in shape, each side measuring approximately 1½km. It is less than 100m at the highest point. Temperatures average 21° C in winter and 26° C in summer. The day we visited the Great Barrier Reef was uncomfortably hot, but on Bedarra it was always pleasant. We had our own secluded bungalow, with ceiling fans but no air conditioning, and it was perfectly comfortable. Mind you, I was 35 years younger then. The food was excellent and alcohol was pour-your-own, bottomless glasses of any liquor your heart desired.

We flew to Dunk Island from Townsville, then took the water taxi to Bedarra. We went to Bedarra in 1983 not primarily for the birds, but just for a holiday. We liked it so much that we returned in 1984. The Hideaway resort we stayed at has not operated since 1991, and it was replaced by another tourist centre, imaginatively called 'the Beddara Resort'. This was destroyed by Cyclone Yasi in 2011, but it has been rebuilt and certainly sounds more luxurious than it was when we were there. There are also private houses available for holiday bookings.

Many Great Barrier Reef islands suffer from lack of water. Bedarra not only has six natural springs, but also enjoys above average rainfall, resulting in lush vegetation. I remember Quandongs with blue fruits, wattles and eucalypts, Beach Hibiscus and Barbed Lawyer Vines. The ancient *Calophyllum* trees look like something out of a magic forest. The local *Melaleucas* don pale yellow flowers twice a year that have a very strong smell of treacle. Birds lap it up to the point of inebriation. There are stories of drunken drongos attacking hapless visitors. There are also horrible Green Ants and gorgeous Ulysses Butterflies, the emblem of Dunk. I remember seeing an echidna, which for some long-forgotten reason we christened Barbette. We'd been told there was nothing toxic on the island, and I believed this to be true until I saw a Death Adder near the dining room. On another occasion

My necklace, a tangible memory of Bedarra.

some litter in the water was mistaken for some sort of stonefish. I should add that litter was just about unheard of on Bedarra – probably much rarer than stonefish. I collected dozens of doughnut-shaped shells, and graded them in size and threaded them to make a necklace, a tangible memory of Bedarra I have to this day.

As I said, we weren't there primarily for the birds, but of course they were the first thing I noted. Orange-footed Scrubfowl tended their mounds, and flocks of Torresian Imperial Pigeons flew over at dawn and dusk. These birds roost on islands and commute to the mainland to feed during the day.

I recall going to see Australian Swiftlets nesting in their cave. We called them Grey Swiftlets in those days, and they are also sometimes called White-rumped Swiftlets, but the IOC, in its inscrutable wisdom, prefers 'Australian Swiftlet'. There are two races of Australian Swiftlet: one on the mainland, centred around Chilligoe (called appropriately *chillagoensis*), and one on the east coast from Mackay to Iron Range (called *terraereginae*). It is this latter race that breeds on Bedarra. It wasn't an easy stroll to get to the swiftlets' cave. We took a boat ride, then clambered over big boulders. We had to jump from rock to rock, and every boulder wobbled beneath our feet. Along the way we saw some spectacular orange orchids. The swiftlets make cheeping noises and navigate their way around their dark cave by echolocation. Their nests were made mainly from grass, cemented together with saliva and stuck to the cave wall. Each tiny nest had one tiny egg. I counted 30 active nests plus some old ones without eggs. Unsurprisingly, there is a very high mortality rate among the birds.

I saw my first Pacific Baza on Bedarra. I called it a Crested Hawk in those days. What a strange, striped, crested raptor it was. He flew above me quite low – I think

I saw my first Pacific Baza on Bedarra.

Brahminy Kites were hanging around the jetty.

he was curious. There were also handsome Brahminy Kites hanging around the jetty (at the time we called them Rufous-backed Sea Eagles) and regal White-bellied Sea Eagles flying past. Young sea eagles were easily confused with Eastern Ospreys, which were also present.

I've seen Sacred Kingfishers on more islands than any other bird. I've seen them from Ashmore Reef to Three Hummock Island, and from Norfolk Island to Boigu – and of course they were on Bedarra. They have a very wide distribution because they are migratory, highly adaptive and have a high reproductive rate, raising two clutches of from three to six chicks each year.

Being from Victoria I was familiar with White-winged Trillers, which visit us every summer, but I saw my very first Varied Triller on Bedarra. I noted his white eyebrow and rust-coloured vent. I also recorded my first Tawny Grassbird here. I saw Dusky and Mangrove Honeyeaters, but dipped on Varied and Yellow-tinted Honeyeaters. Blue-winged Kookaburras uttered their maniacal calls and Spangled Drongos made weird rasping and crackling noises.

Friends I recognized from home included Rufous Fantails, Rainbow Bee-eaters and Mistletoebirds. My favourite woodswallows, White-breasted, were present every day, bombing the Brahminy Kite if he left his jetty and invaded their territory. There were Rose-crowned Fruit Doves and Pacific Emerald Doves, and we could watch Brown Boobies out at sea, beautiful silhouettes in the sunset.

Sacred Kingfishers are on more islands than any other bird.

Blue-winged Kookaburras made their maniacal calls.

It is a long time since I was on Bedarra and it's fascinating how many bird names have changed. The bird list I was using was compiled by E. J. Banfield from his time living on Dunk Island from 1897 until 1923. If I thought there's been far too many name changes in the last 30 years, Banfield's list of names has lots of enigmatic confusions for today's birder. Some names I don't recognize at all. I could perhaps guess that a Black-headed Diamond-bird was a Striated Pardalote and, at a stretch, that a Yellow-necked Mangrove Bittern was a Black Bittern. However, I don't think I'd have ever discovered by myself that a Varied Graucalus Cuckooshrike was a White-bellied Cuckooshrike (we used to call it Little Cuckooshrike), that a Long-billed Stone-plover was a Beach Stone-curlew, or that a Fasciated Honeyeater was a Mangrove Honeyeater. Other odd names were Pectoral Rail for Buff-banded Rail, Shining Calornis Starling for Metallic Starling and Jardine Caterpillar-eater for Common Cicadabird. What, I wonder, was an Allied Pigeon? I haven't yet figured that out.

For me, Bedarra will always mean sunbirds, pittas, swiftlets and Large-tailed Nightjars. The beaches, butterflies and turquoise seas are picture-book perfect, but I will always remember the Pacific Baza flying down to investigate me, and the unexpected beauty of a Spectacled Monarch. I would like to return to Bedarra. The words 'tropical paradise' have quite possibly lost impact through overuse; nevertheless I can think of no better description for Bedarra. It is truly a tropical paradise.

Friends from home included Rufous Fantails.

My favourite woodswallow, the White-breasted, was present every day.

20 Lord Howe Island

Birders must go to Lord Howe Island to see the woodhen.

KEY SPECIES

- White-bellied Storm Petrel
- Providence Petrel
- Kermadec Petrel
- Black-winged Petrel
- Wedge-tailed Shearwater
- Flesh-footed Shearwater
- Little Shearwater
- Red-tailed Tropicbird
- Masked Booby
- Lord Howe Woodhen
- Pacific Golden Plover
- Brown Noddy
- Black Noddy
- Grey Noddy
- White Tern
- Sooty Tern
- Australian Masked Owl
- Lord Howe race of
  Australian Golden Whistler

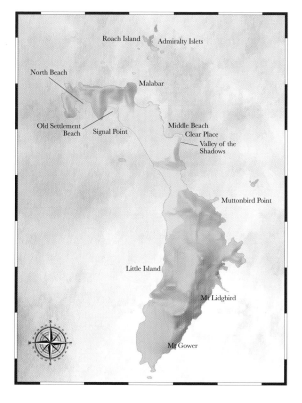

Right: Lord Howe Island.

You can see Providence Petrels on east-coast pelagics, as well as Flesh-footed and Wedge-tailed Shearwaters. You can see Sooty Terns, Brown Noddies (previously called Common Noddies) and Red-tailed Tropicbirds on Christmas Island. You can see White Terns on Cocos (Keeling) Islands, and Masked Boobies and Black Noddies on Ashmore Reef. I don't believe I've ever seen Black-winged Petrels or Little Shearwaters anywhere except on Lord Howe Island, but it is at least theoretically possible to do so. Black-winged Petrels can supposedly be seen on east-coast pelagics, and Little Shearwaters are reputedly seen off south-west Western Australia. I saw Grey Noddies (otherwise known as Grey Ternlets) on Norfolk Island as well as on Lord Howe Island. They can also be seen on Lady Elliot Island or North Stradbroke Island, or on a Southport pelagic. But a Lord Howe Woodhen can only be seen running wild on Lord Howe Island.

Despite having World Heritage listing, Lord Howe Island has the dubious distinction of having more extinct birds than any other Australian island. It has had five species and five subspecies declared extinct. The species are: the White-throated Pigeon, Pycroft's Petrel, White Gallinule, Lord Howe Gerygone and Robust White-eye. The subspecies are: the Tasman Parakeet (the race on Norfolk Island is Critically Endangered), Southern Boobook (persists on the mainland), Grey Fantail

Lord Howe Woodhen.

(persists on the mainland), Island Thrush (also extinct on Norfolk Island, but persists on Christmas Island in Australian territory, as well as on several Pacific islands and in Southeast Asia), and Tasman Starling (also extinct on Norfolk Island, so the species is also extinct).

Lord Howe Island lies 600km east of the Australian mainland in the Tasman Sea. Ball's Pyramid is 23km to the south-east and the Admiralty Group is immediately to the north, the largest islet in the group being Roach Island. Norfolk Island lies a further 800km to the north-east. Lord Howe Island comprises about 1,500ha and has a population of 350 people. Two mountains dominate the island: Mt Gower (87m) and Mt Lidgbird (77m). Visitors with nothing better to do climb Mt Gower. I didn't do it, so I don't know how dangerous it is. On the west of the island there is a sheltered lagoon, defined by the world's most southern coral reef. My memory of the island is of day lilies, golden orb spiders and ethereal White Terns. I also recall my wobbly attempts to ride a bike, magnificent Red-tailed Tropicbirds, Kentia Palms, Pacific Golden Plovers in full breeding plumage, very friendly Brown Noddies, and of course the wonderful woodhen.

When I visited Lord Howe Island, the story of the Lord Howe Woodhen was nothing short of inspirational. Today, the woodhen's future is again under a shadow. Early

My memory of Lord Howe is of ethereal White Terns.

One of the magnificent Red-tailed Tropicbirds.

This Pacific Golden Plover is moulting out of breeding plumage.

settlers dined on woodhens, as did cats and pigs, and their habitat was destroyed by feral pigs and goats. Because of these factors, in the 1970s the population of woodhens crashed to fewer than 10 breeding pairs. Following a successful captive-breeding programme, the population today has reached the island's estimated carrying capacity of 220 individuals. However, now there is competition from Buff-banded Rails. These birds were said to have been introduced to the island in the nineteenth century, but they could well have colonized it by themselves. Their population has fluctuated and recent increases lead some ornithologists to conclude that they recolonized the island at some time after the 1970s.

Rats have been a problem on Lord Howe Island since they were accidentally introduced in 1918. Efforts were made to keep the island free of rats. In those days ships were required to anchor offshore and transfer cargo to the island by small boats. This worked well until the captain of the SS *Makambo* collapsed. The crew was distracted and the ship ran aground. The ship was beached for nine days, giving the rats ample opportunity to disembark. A hundred years later, in winter 2018, a rodent-eradication programme will take place. The plan is to take the entire population of woodhens and currawongs into captivity while rat poison is laid systematically

Masked Booby – some people want these split as Tasman Boobies.

throughout the island. Rats and mice have been eradicated successfully from other islands, so Lord Howe can hope to be rat free in the very near future.

Roger and I visited Lord Howe Island in March 1996 and I recorded 31 bird species, including the local races of Silvereye, Pied Currawong and Australian Golden Whistler. Some people believe that the local race of Masked Booby should be given species status, called the Tasman Booby.

We arrived on Saturday. The first bird we saw was a Magpie-lark. On Sunday we hired bikes and admired White Tern chicks being cared for at the bike-hire shop. White Terns do not build a nest, but lay their single egg on a bare branch. Consequently, there are many fatalities, and many chicks fall off their perches.

On Sunday afternoon we visited Muttonbird Point to see Masked Boobies. The wind was very strong beside the airstrip, making my incompetent bike riding even more difficult. We left our bikes in a rack and tackled the walk up a large hill, which was supposed to take 45 minutes, but which was hard work and took much longer. Along the way we saw rats and Pacific Emerald Doves. There were lots of Brown Noddies and the Masked Boobies had young. We also saw Red-tailed Tropicbirds and a lone Sooty Tern. We found the ride back to our lodging very hard work, and I'd lost faith in my ability to ride a bike. That evening after tea we took our torches and went looking for owls along the airport fenceposts. We didn't see any.

We were looking for Australian Masked Owls. The endemic subspecies of Southern Boobook was sadly extinct, but Australian Masked Owls had been introduced in the 1920s in a rather ill-considered attempt to control rats. The owls found seabird and woodhen chicks much easier to catch then pesky rats, and dined on Black-winged and Providence Petrels, White Terns and endangered woodhens. We went spotlighting on two further occasions, but saw no owls at all.

On Monday morning we went to Malabar for Red-tailed Tropicbirds. We thought this would be an easy walk after our exertion the previous day walking to Muttonbird Point, but it was not. I thought the fluffy tropicbird chicks made it worthwhile; I'm not sure if Rog did.

At lunchtime a female Lord Howe Golden Whistler entered the guest house dining room, unnoticed except by me. People at the next table had a copy of Ian Hutton's book, *Birds of Lord Howe Island,* and were chatting about the birds they would see. If they couldn't see the whistler, I wasn't sure how they'd go with the seabirds. The whistler was evidently quite at home, hopping on to an adjacent table and pecking the butter. I don't think it was the first time it had visited this dining room.

Providence Petrels are not exclusive to Lord Howe Island.

I thought I saw Black-winged Petrels and I probably did.

In the afternoon we decided to visit Little Island and look for woodhens. I was already quite sick of this cycling silliness, so we decided to take the bus. We waited and waited, but no bus came. Reluctantly, we set off again on our bikes. We rode over three cattle grids and my poor sore bottom felt every bump. I reckoned I'd earned woodhens, but we didn't see any. We did see thousands of Providence Petrels. We shouted at them but they did not land beside us as we'd been led to expect.

We returned to Little Island on Tuesday morning and this time I saw one elusive woodhen. Rog saw more beside the first cattle grid, but I was too busy hanging on to my handlebars to look around. We had sore hands from clapping to attract woodhens. It didn't work. I was past caring. I'd seen one bird. The Lord Howe Woodhen was irrevocably on my life list.

In the afternoon we visited Old Settlement Beach and the museum that my notes report cost A$2 and was 'just about worth it'. Then we did a joy flight around the island and Ball's Pyramid. I had wanted to do a boat trip to Ball's Pyramid, but strong winds from a northern cyclone prohibited boats from doing anything other than hugging the shoreline, so the joy flight was our compromise. We were in a

Cessna 173 and taking photos through the tiny Perspex windows was difficult. I thought I saw both Kermadec and Black-winged Petrels (and I probably did) but without the presence of someone better at identifying seabirds than I am, I felt I could not, in all honesty, count either bird.

At 4.45 a.m. on Wednesday, in the pitch dark, very bravely by myself, I visited Blinky Beach looking for Wedge-tailed Shearwaters. These birds breed on Lord Howe Island from September to April. In March I expected chicks to be in the burrows and adults to fly out to sea to feed early in the morning. I thought I'd catch them leaving. I didn't see any. These are not rare birds and I've seen them many times off Wollongong, where they are very common from October to April.

Later we did a boat trip to North Beach, where we saw lots of confiding Brown Noddies on the rocky shore.

On Thursday we walked to Clear Place, Valley of the Shadows and Middle Beach. We saw lots of shearwater burrows, but no birds. In the afternoon we did a guided walk to Little Island, and this time, with the benefit of a guide, we saw lots of woodhens. The guide told us that there were five different palms on Lord Howe, as well as a banyan that spreads over an acre, a native rosemary and Lignum Vitae. Then he climbed a palm tree to show us how (or to show off, depending on your point of view). Up the palm tree he gathered witchetty grubs to feed to the woodhens. He yelled at the petrels – a noise rather like the one we used to make when playing cowboys and Indians when we were kids. It worked. Petrels flopped through the vegetation and he picked one up.

Before breakfast on Friday we went to Signal Point. We did a boat trip in the morning, which was rather curtailed because of the cyclone up north. The seas were quite rough but I sat at the front nevertheless to see the birds. I saw Grey and Black Noddies, as well as flying Garfish and a huge giant ray. In the afternoon we did a bus tour of the island. At dusk we rode our bikes to Signal Point to see Wedge-tailed Shearwaters returning to Rabbit Island.

With great glee we returned our bikes to the hire shop. I have not ridden a bike since and can assert with complete confidence that I never will again. We walked to Middle Beach to see Black-winged Petrels and Flesh-footed Shearwaters from the beach. We could also see Little Shearwaters on the Admiralty Islets.

We left on Saturday, disappointed that we hadn't been able to do a boat trip around Ball's Pyramid, but quite pleased with our bird list nevertheless. We'd dipped on the owl, Kermadec Petrel and White-bellied Storm Petrel, but I consoled myself with the thought that 16 out of 19 is not too bad.

Black Noddies are not exclusive to Lord Howe Island.

At dusk, we watched Wedge-tailed Shearwaters return to Rabbit Island.

21 Norfolk Island

*Norfolk Island has its own parrot, robin, warbler and white-eye.
It's also perhaps the easiest place in Australia to see the California
Quail. Don't believe the tourist handouts: you cannot count the
feral geese. So birders travelling to Norfolk Island can expect to
add four birds to their life total, or five if the California Quail isn't
already on their list. The quail can also be found on King Island,
but the other four can only be seen on Norfolk Island. There are
also local races of the Grey Fantail and Australian Golden Whistler.*

KEY SPECIES

- California Quail
- Providence Petrel
- Masked Booby
- Grey Noddy
- Norfolk Parakeet
- Norfolk Gerygone

- Norfolk Robin
- Slender-billed White-eye

Local races of:
- Australian Golden Whistler
- Grey Fantail

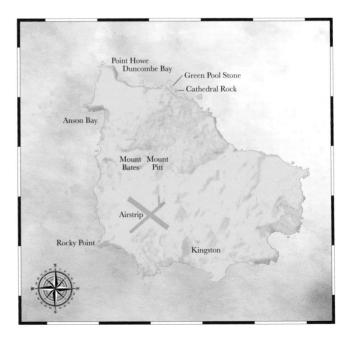

Right: Norfolk Island.

Norfolk Island's record of avian extinctions is second only to that of Lord Howe Island. Two species are extinct: the Norfolk Ground Dove and the Norfolk Island Kaka. One species has been extirpated from Norfolk Island, although it still breeds on several New Zealand islands and is a vagrant to Australia: that is Pycroft's Petrel. Four subspecies have gone extinct on Norfolk: the Norfolk Island race of the New Zealand Pigeon (still found in New Zealand), Long-tailed Triller (still found on New Caledonia, Vanuatu and the Solomons), Island Thrush (also extinct on Lord Howe Island, but persists on Christmas Island and other Pacific islands, as well as in Southeast Asia), and the Tasman Starling (also extinct on Lord Howe Island, so the species, too, is extinct). As if this wasn't enough, there is also the White-chested White-eye, which is listed as 'Critically Endangered (possibly Extinct)'. This bird has most likely been extinct since 1979. Several determined surveys have failed to find it. It was last seen in the Mt Pitt Reserve.

Norfolk Island is located 1,000km to the east of mainland Australia, 1,670km east-north-east of Sydney. It is probably easiest to think of it as lying between New Zealand and New Caledonia. The island comprises 3,850ha, measures 8 x 5km and has more than 30km of coastline. There are two tiny uninhabited islands to the south: Nepean Island, 1km away, and Philip Island, 6km away. At roughly 2 x 2km wide, Philip Island is the larger of the two and rises to 280m above sea level. The Norfolk Island National Park covers 650ha, including 190ha on Philip Island and 5.5ha in the Norfolk Island Botanic Garden. Pests on Norfolk Island include cats, rats and mice, although these have been eradicated from Philip Island. I admired a pretty Hawaiian Holly with bright red berries until I learnt that it was an unwelcome and ubiquitous weed. I also remember a very attractive native hibiscus.

Norfolk Islanders appear proud of their mutinous history – a bit like Australians being excited to find a convict on their family tree. Norfolk Island was uninhabited when Captain Cook discovered it in 1774, and England established it as a penal settlement in 1788. When this colony dissolved in 1814, a quarter of the island's vegetation had been destroyed. A second penal colony was established in 1825 and lasted until 1856. During both these settlements the island's iconic pines were cut down, and cattle, sheep, pigs, goats and chickens were introduced. At that time the survivors of the mutiny on the *Bounty* were living on Pitcairn Island. When Norfolk Island was no longer required as a gaol, Queen Victoria granted it to the Pitcairners, who translocated to the island, bringing their Tahitian wives with them.

Norfolk Island has its own time zone, an hour and a half ahead of Australian Eastern Standard Time, but the television operates on mainland time, so any 8.30

Philip Island is 6km to the south.

Hawaiian Holly Schinus terebinthifolius,
pretty but a weed nonetheless.

Philip Island Hibiscus.

evening programme does not commence until 10 p.m. The whole place closes down on Wednesday afternoons.

The climate is called subtropical temperate. Summer temperatures vary between 19° C and 28° C; winter temperatures between 12° C and 22° C. Roger and I were there for a week in July 2004 and it rained every day. The day we arrived, 579 other visitors arrived too. At peak times the island accommodates 1,000 visitors. The resident population is 1,800 people. For an island so dependent on tourism, Norfolk has a lot to learn about welcoming visitors. It's all very well for drivers to wave at each other, but a friendly smile and good service in the shops and cafes would be much more welcoming.

During our visit cows wandered freely on the very poorly maintained roads, and there were lots of feral chickens and geese. My notes say that cows and ducks have right of way, but chickens do not. Why should ducks be more important than chickens? As I said, the locals are very proud of their *Bounty* mutineer heritage and, while English is the official language, the locals speak Pitcairn. The island is very neat, with many mown lawns and no litter. However, there are no footpaths, something that makes walking difficult. There are pretty butterflies and lots of golden orb spiders.

It seems that everyone living on Norfolk Island has a nickname, and all these names are printed in the local phone book. Several birds have nicknames too. Wedge-tailed Shearwaters are called Ghost Birds, and Little Shearwaters are called Laro. Australasian Swamphens are Tarler Birds and, confusingly, both Buff-banded Rails and Spotless Crakes are called Little Tarler Birds. Pacific Golden Plovers are called Snipe – luckily there are no snipe on Norfolk. Whimbrels are called Shipmate, and Black Noddies are called either Titerack or Tetrach. Silvereyes and both White-chested and Slender-billed White-eyes are all called Grinells indiscriminately. Australian Golden Whistlers are called Tamey.

Providence Petrels breed on Philip Island. Formerly they bred on Norfolk Island itself, but when supply ships did not arrive the early settlers dined on petrels (hence the birds were regarded as providential), reportedly killing more than 170,000 birds and causing their local extinction. Gould named the birds *Pterodroma solandri* after the Swedish naturalist Dr D. C. Solander, who was on Cook's voyage in the *Endeavour* from 1768 to 1771, which discovered Norfolk. Today, New South Wales birders insist on calling them Solander's Petrels, but I stick with the IOC and call them Providence Petrels. I like this name as every time I use it, I'm reminded of man's stupidity. If Providence Petrels hadn't been present on Philip or Lord Howe Islands, this bird may now have been extinct. How providential would that be?

Black Noddies, locally called either Titerack or Tetrach.

Providence Petrel.

We arrived on a Sunday and saw Norfolk Gerygones at Kingston that afternoon. We saw Crimson Rosellas, Sacred Kingfishers, Grey Fantails and Song Thrushes every day.

The Norfolk Gerygone, a warbler endemic to Norfolk Island.

Sacred Kingfishers were very common on the island.

We saw the Song Thrush every day.

On Tuesday we did the Summit Walk along the ridge from Mt Pitt to Mt Bates before breakfast. At 318m, Mt Bates is the island's highest point, only just ahead of Mt Pitt at 316m. We were hoping for Norfolk Parakeets, at that time called Red-crowned Parakeets, and sometimes known as Tasman Parakeets. The locals call them Green Parrots to distinguish them from Red Parrots, their name for introduced Crimson Rosellas. Norfolk Parakeets are Critically Endangered. The population is perhaps 250 mature adults, and it may be declining. Although we didn't see any parakeets, we did see Norfolk Robins (at that time classified as a race of the Scarlet Robin, but since upgraded to species status), and the Norfolk Island race of the Australian Golden Whistler, which isn't golden at all.

At Green Pool Stone in the Northern Islets, we saw a dozen Masked Boobies nesting. One pair changed nest duty and we saw two beautiful brown splotchy eggs. Two is the normal clutch but usually only one chick is raised successfully. Many people believe these boobies should be split and called Tasman Boobies.

Masked Boobies usually raise only one chick.

I wanted to look for seabirds but it was always too wet to stand around in the rain. I did see Grey Noddies flying around Cathedral Rock. We walked from the 100 Acre Reserve to Rocky Point and got our shoes caked in red sticky mud, but we did manage to see Slender-billed White-eyes. After two days on the island, we'd seen all our target species except the parakeet and the quail.

I saw Grey Noddies flying around Cathedral Rock.

The Slender-billed White-eye is endemic to Norfolk Island.

Early on Wednesday morning we walked from Mt Pitt to Palm Glen, again looking for Norfolk Parakeets. It rained and few birds put in an appearance. We were wet and miserable and fearing that we may never see the parakeets, when suddenly we heard the call. *Kek kek kek,* they said, sounding like the beginning of a Laughing Kookaburra's guffaw. Suddenly the rain didn't matter. I was going to see the parakeets. It took some time and my optimism had waned, when at last there they were. We had great views. Our wet clothes were no longer of any consequence. We'd seen all the endemics. Only the plastic quail to go.

We were flying out on Saturday and we'd visited all the recommended birdy spots. I didn't have a clue where to look for the quail, so I rang the National Park Office and asked them. I was told to drive along Duncombe Bay Road and look for the quail from the car. We did this and ticked the quail at Point Howe. We watched a pair of the birds walking under a pine tree. I expected the male to be showy, but the female was unexpectedly beautiful.

I'd now seen everything I'd expected to see and had two full days left to concentrate on a bird that was probably extinct, the afore-mentioned White-chested White-eye (sometimes called the White-breasted White-eye). The last confirmed sighting was four records during an intense survey in 1979, although there had been a few unconfirmed reports since then. Amateurs' sightings are not readily accepted because the birds looks so similar to Silvereyes and Slender-billed White-eyes, both of which are on Norfolk. You really need a photograph or the presence of an expert if you are to be believed. We looked at Palm Glen, then 100 Acre Reserve. Needless to say, we did not see the bird. However, we did meet Margaret Christian, chair of the local Fauna and Flora Society and well-known local birding expert.

We left early on Saturday afternoon and were farewelled with the words 'Yorlye Cum Back Suun', which we were told meant, 'Everyone come back soon'. My lasting memory of Norfolk is of statuesque pine trees festooned with lichen, like tinsel on a Christmas tree, and lots of pretty views and interesting plants, but generally very few birds.

We finally saw Norfolk Parakeets at Palm Glen.

California Quail were present on Duncombe Bay Road.

22 Cabbage Tree Island

Until quite recently Cabbage Tree Island was the only known nesting site of Australia's rarest endemic seabird, Gould's Petrel. I sought permission from the New South Wales Parks and Wildlife Service to visit Cabbage Tree Island, and was refused. This is the third island in this book on which I have not set foot (see page 7).

KEY SPECIES

• Gould's Petrel

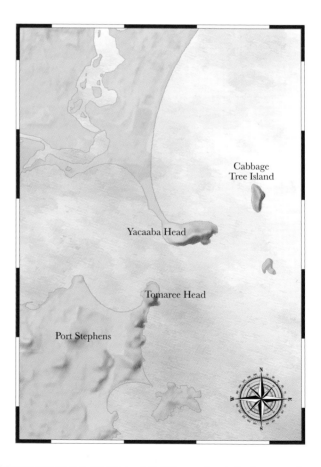

Right: Cabbage Tree Island with Wedge-tailed Shearwaters in the foreground..

Cabbage Tree Island is just outside Port Stephens harbour, 1.4km east of the north head called Yacaaba, some 160km north of Sydney. There are three small islands just outside the heads: Cabbage Tree Island to the north, Little Boondelbah to the east and Boondelbah to the south. Broughton Island (14ha) is 18km further north of the heads. All four islands lie within the Port Stephens-Great Lakes Marine Park.

Cabbage Tree Island comprises 26.3ha of rocky cliffs, *Lomandra* grassland and subtropical rainforest. Interestingly, this is the only rainforest found offshore in south-eastern Australia. The island is about 1km from north to south and 480m at its widest point. The highest point is 123m above sea level. On the island's seaward side, steep, rocky cliffs make landing impossible, and there are no sandy beaches on the island. Its western side is steep and rocky too, but there is a sloping rock shelf suitable for landing when conditions are calm. This side of the island is well vegetated, particularly the two gullies, imaginatively called North Gully and South Gully. There are some quite large trees here – figs, native plums, as well as the eponymous Cabbage Tree Palms. These can grow to more than 12m high. There are also Bird-lime Trees – famous for entrapping birds. There are *Banksias* at the island's southern end. In fact there are more than 150 plant species on the island. A rocky outcrop on the east of the island known as Cathedral Rock is home to nesting Peregrine Falcons.

The island was a sanctuary controlled by the New South Wales Fauna and Flora Protection Board until 1954, when it was declared the John Gould Faunal Reserve under the control of the New South Wales National Parks and Wildlife Service. This was the first faunal reserve in New South Wales and was established to protect Gould's Petrels. Under the National Parks and Wildlife Act 1967, all faunal reserves became nature reserves. Nature reserves differ from national parks because they have no public access and hence no visitor facilities. Nature reserves are proclaimed to protect nature, not to provide a glimpse of wilderness for curious city dwellers, hence the lack of public access. This is why my request to visit the island was refused. It is no doubt a good thing that access is not easier. It is a very enticing little island, quite close to shore, and if there were inviting sandy beaches it would be difficult to keep people away. Perhaps the slippery sloping rocks on the west side and the steep rugged cliffs on the east are the island's best protection – and the best protection for Gould's Petrel.

Waters to the north, east and south of Cabbage Tree Island are a declared sanctuary and fishing is not allowed. To the west of the island, fishing is permitted for bait only.

Gould's Petrel is listed as Vulnerable on the World Conservation Union (formerly the IUCN) Red List. It has been declared Endangered under the Environment Protection and Biodiversity Conservation Act 1999, and listed as Vulnerable under

Cabbage Tree Island hosts the only rainforest found offshore in south-eastern Australia.

Australia's rarest endemic seabird, Gould's Petrel, breeds on Cabbage Tree Island.

the New South Wales Threatened Species Conservation Act 1995. It was previously listed as Endangered. What's more, Gould's Petrel is the only New South Wales bird to have achieved a downgraded conservation status. It was Endangered in 1990, then downgraded to Vulnerable in 2000 and remained Vulnerable in 2010. The reason for this downgrading is, put most simply, improvement in the bird's habitat. Of course there was nothing simple about it. It took many years of dedicated work by several expert ornithologists supported by many enthusiastic volunteers. It involved eradication of rabbits from Cabbage Tree Island, killing predators that preyed on vulnerable chicks and adults, and removing Bird-lime Trees. When the petrel's plight first became obvious, there was only one known breeding colony – a potentially very dangerous circumstance. Removal of rodents on a nearby island allowed translocation of chicks to form a second colony. Moreover, I don't think it was a coincidence that removal of rodents from other nearby islands was quickly followed by Gould's Petrels nesting there too. Today, there are four known nesting locations.

Without a doubt the person who knew Cabbage Tree Island better than anyone else was Athel D'Ombrain. Affectionately known as Dommy, Athel D'Ombrain was a big-game fisherman and photographer, a keen naturalist and an amateur ornithologist. He started visiting Cabbage Tree Island in 1930 and began banding the petrels in 1948. During the Second World War, when the island was used for artillery practice, Dommy was instrumental in stopping it. In 1964 he banded his 400th Gould's Petrel. He was careful not to mark where nests were located so as not to assist predators in finding chicks. He was bemused that no chick he banded was ever recovered. When he died in 1985, the population of Gould's Petrels was estimated to be around 200 breeding pairs.

Until 1989 there had not been a proper census of the Gould's Petrel breeding colony on Cabbage Tree Island. All that we know is that the birds were said to be abundant in John Gould's day, some 175 years ago. Accurate counts are difficult because of the hilly, rocky terrain, and because the birds' nests are hidden beneath the rocks and palm fronds. In 1970 it was thought that there were somewhere around 250–500 breeding pairs, and breeding success was 40 per cent. In 1989 the National Parks and Wildlife Service commissioned the Commonwealth Scientific and Industrial Research Organisation (CSIRO) to undertake a survey. This found that there were fewer than 300 breeding pairs, which is within the 250–500 range, but what was of concern was that only 25 per cent of eggs produced young. In 1992 there were fewer than 250 pairs, a significant reduction in just three years. The population was in decline. More birds were dying than being hatched. What had gone wrong on Cabbage Tree Island? The 1992 report commissioned to identify the problem gave a simple three-pronged answer: 1. *Pisonia*; 2. Pied Currawongs and 3. Australian Ravens. It also noted the presence of pest plants, namely prickly pears (*Opuntia*) and the Bitou Bush.

In truth, while there were several pressures on the petrel population, the single underlying cause was the rabbit *Oryctolagus cuniculus*. Rabbits ate the undergrowth, so new trees could not establish. This made the island more susceptible to weeds, and with no new palms, figs or native plums being established, over time the entire ecosystem was changing. There was a danger that south-eastern Australia's only offshore subtropical rainforest would be

The main problem was the rabbit.

lost. Sticky *Pisonia* seeds that would naturally fall and be entangled in the undergrowth now fell to the ground, where petrels, both adults and chicks, were immobilized by the seeds fouling their feathers and sticking their wings to their bodies. These birds inevitably died, either from starvation or from predation. Without undergrowth there was nowhere for petrels to shelter from predators. What's more, the presence of rabbits attracted more predators.

The major avian predators were Pied Currawongs and Australian Ravens, but there were also resident Peregrine Falcons, possible Laughing Kookaburras and occasional visits from Grey Goshawks, Brown Falcons, and Barking and Powerful Owls. Currawongs were not a problem on the island in Dommy's day, but with increased urbanization along the coast the currawong population exploded. Pied Currawongs nest in spring. In January, just when Gould's Petrels hatch, the currawongs are out hunting for food for their ravenous young. In fact these clever birds learnt to systematically quarter the petrels' nesting colonies searching for seabird chicks. A defenceless fledgling was easily dispatched and shoved into a fork in a branch, where it was dismembered and fed to hungry currawong babies. Currawongs killed adults and chicks alike. In the summer of 1992–1993, 52 dead adult petrels were found. Of these, 42 had been killed by currawongs.

Pied Currawongs are a very successful, very adaptable species. They are omnivorous, eating just about everything from fruits and berries to roadkill, and from worms and snails to baby possums, and birds and their eggs. Before European settlement Pied Currawongs bred in summer in the mountains and spent the winter on the coastal plains. Today there is so much food available along the urban coast that they are resident there all year round. They no longer bother to trek to higher ground in summer. It is the European berry-producing trees that Australians have planted in their gardens that feed the currawongs in the warmer months. They like the berries of privet, firethorn, hawthorn and Camphor Laurel. They eat the pulp and regurgitate the seeds in pellets, thus spreading these exotic plants into the native bush. The population of Pied Currawongs is abundant and increasing. We rarely saw them when I was a child growing up in suburban Melbourne. Today I can see them in my garden in suburban Melbourne every day of the year.

Australian Ravens are also abundant, but their population has not exploded in the same way that the Pied Currawong numbers have. Like currawongs, ravens are clever, adaptable birds. In years gone by farmers blamed them for killing lambs, but ravens do not kill healthy lambs. They will kill a lamb that is sickly, and of course they will prey on any dead animal, including lambs. I believe they have learnt to eat carrion, and that before European settlement Australian Ravens dined predominantly on live prey. Now they are mainly carnivorous, but they will also clean up any rubbish left lying about, including dead animals and uneaten pizza. They are particularly clever at finding other birds' nests, and will eat both eggs and nestlings.

Thus in the early 1990s people began to realize that the Gould's Petrels were in trouble. Rabbits had eaten the undergrowth. Petrels had nowhere to hide from currawongs and ravens, and the effect of *Pisonia* seeds was being exacerbated. Things did not look good – and, ultimately, it was all thanks to the bunny.

Is there any other cute, furry herbivore that has caused so much economic damage and endangered so many species? Today, according to the New South Wales government, rabbits cost Australian agriculture A$115 million per annum – and that's after countless millions have been spent on myxomatosis, calicivirus, fumigation, poisoning and digging up warrens. They are a worldwide environmental problem, but how did they get to Cabbage Tree Island?

After rabbits were introduced to the Australian mainland in 1859, they spread very quickly. By 1900 they had become a major environmental problem costing the agricultural industry millions of pounds per annum. In 1905 the New South Wales government offered a reward of £25,000 (around A$3,430,000 today – not bad for a state government reward) for a method of eradicating the expensive pest. At the same time the New South Wales Minister for Lands communicated with the Pasteur Institute in Paris, seeking advice about biological control of rabbits. Dr Jean Danysz (1860–1928), a Polish pathologist, was working at the Pasteur Institute at the time. He had developed a strain of bacteria that, he said, would kill feral rabbits but do no harm to other living creatures. The Minister for Lands asked Dr Danysz to come to Australia and prove his case. No doubt Dr Danysz was attracted by the £25,000 reward. However, there was a great deal of public alarm about the release of this new bacterium into the wild, and when Dr Danysz arrived he was asked to confine his experiments to the laboratory until it was confirmed that the bacterium could not harm anything other than rabbits. The Danysz Rabbit Inoculation Station was established on Broughton Island, situated 18km from the mainland off Port Stephens and presumably considered sufficiently remote to quell public alarm. As part of Dr Danysz's experiments, rabbits were released on Cabbage Tree Island in 1906. Perhaps in 1906 one small, uninhabited island off Port Stephens was thought to qualify as 'a laboratory'. With the wonderful benefit of hindsight it's a shame that the public alarm was not louder and more prolonged. In the end Dr Danysz was proved at least partly correct: his bacterium did not affect other creatures. However, it did not kill all the rabbits either.

Pied Currawongs were identified as a major problem.

Laughing Kookaburras might also have posed a threat to Gould's Petrels.

Other predators included Peregrine Falcons.

Australian Ravens were another problem.

It took many years for rabbits to become a major environmental problem on Cabbage Tree Island. Certainly, Dommy did not regard them as a serious concern, and as recently as 1976 Peter Fullagar did not regard the rabbit as a major disaster. He reported that numbers were small and the rabbit's influence was unstudied and unknown. In 1997 the population of rabbits on Cabbage Tree Island was estimated to be 250 – a number remarkably similar to the population of Gould's Petrels at that time. Fullagar did a vegetation survey and noted that efforts had been made to remove prickly pears. He did not mention the Bitou Bush, so we must assume that this weed arrived after 1976. It established itself primarily on the south-east of the island, but there were also patches on the cliffs to the north and east.

I remember being taught about prickly pears at primary school. They were supposed to be a good example of effective biological pest control, although so many prickly pears remain around the countryside today that one may be permitted to question whether this really is so. These Mexican cacti were introduced into Australia in the nineteenth century in order to provide a natural agricultural fence and because they was hosts to the cochineal insect, the basis of a red dye industry. The plants were quickly out of control. Realizing their error, farmers tried to plough the plants in, thus exacerbating the problem many fold, as each cut stem grew into a new plant. The Cactus Moth *Cactoblastis cactorum* eats prickly pears. These moths were introduced and in 1925 were regarded as a successful control of the plants.

Prickly pears and the Bitou Bush are unwanted exotic weeds and there is no doubt that Cabbage Tree Island would be better off without them. However, the plant that does most damage to the petrels is a native: it is the Bird-lime Tree *Pisonia umbellifera*. A single sticky fruit from this bush can incapacitate a bird. Attempts to remove fruits are futile, as no matter how much care is taken the sticky residue remains, and birds affected with the fruit will never fly again. The fruits ripen just when the chicks hatch, and fruits retain their sticky coating for months. They are a menace to both fledglings and adults returning to feed their young.

The Bird-lime Tree is so effective in incapacitating birds that various native peoples used these fruits to catch birds. There are many species of *Pisonia* throughout the tropics and subtropics, especially in America and South-east Asia. Australia has three species that grow in Queensland, New South Wales, Northern Territory and Western Australia. A larger tree, *Pisonia grandis*, 18m high with a trunk of 2.5m diameter, is responsible for the deaths of many Black Noddies on Heron Island in the Great Barrier Reef. Here noddies nest in the *Pisonia* trees. Chicks blown out of the nest succumb to the sticky *Pisonia* seeds on the ground. Adults, too, can be trapped by adhesive fruits and this is usually fatal. Piles of dead noddies are removed from view around tourist resorts.

Pisonia umbellifera on Cabbage Tree Island is a smaller plant, more of a shrub than the huge tropical trees further north. In 1941 Hindwood and Serventy reported that:

Mostly small birds are trapped by the sticky seeds, which are somewhat more than an inch in length, narrow and ridged, and exude a very viscid substance. They grow in rather open clusters, which fall to the ground when ripe. It is then that the petrels, making their way down the gullies to the sea, are liable to be entangled in them. The more they struggle the worse grows their plight, and they may become quite helpless when thoroughly caught in the toils of the deadly gluey seeds. Leaves and debris from the forest floor stick to the seeds and the birds' feathers in the struggle, and a gummed bird, so encumbered, would not be able to fly and must slowly starve to death. [...] It seemed to us that most of the Pisonia *trees were growing on the lower slopes and that comparatively few trees, which could be readily removed, were actually in the path of the birds leaving the nesting area.*

Athel D'Ombrain heeded this advice and removed some trees. Luckily, at that time there was no one to tell him not to.

Following the drastic fall in numbers of Gould's Petrels, the New South Wales Department of Environment and Conservation began an active management plan in 1992. The entire island had been closed to the public in 1954 and declared the John Gould Nature Reserve. In 1996 an interim recovery plan was prepared with objectives including controlling numbers of Pied Currawongs and Australian Ravens, removing *Pisonia* trees, eradicating rabbits, monitoring other predators, improving the petrel's breeding success and conducting a local awareness campaign. This work was remarkably successful and the breeding population grew to 1,000 pairs in 2001. Many people helped in this success, but two most noteworthy are David Priddel and Nicholas Carlile. Also worthy of mention are the Cumberland Bird Observers Club and Birds Australia Threatened Bird Network.

So, this small, inaccessible New South Wales island has quite a story to tell. A complex interaction between introduced pests and native vegetation caused unnatural deaths and predation, and very nearly resulted in the demise of one very rare seabird.

Gould's Petrels were translocated to nearby Boondelbah Island and a second colony has been established there successfully. In recent years, following rat eradication, the petrels have also been discovered breeding on Broughton, Little Broughton and Montague Islands. How heart-warming it is to have a good-news conservation story to end on.

Bibliography

Brothers, N., et al. (2001) *Tasmania's Offshore Islands: Seabirds and Other Natural Features*. Tasmanian Museum and Art Gallery. Hobart, Tasmania.

Burbidge, A. A., Marchant, N. G., McKenzie, N. L. & Wilson, P. G. (1978) *Part II – Environment in the Islands of the North-West Kimberley, Western Australia*. Burbidge, A. A. & McKenzie N. L. (eds) Department of Fisheries and Wildlife, Perth.

Chisholm, A. H. & Cayley, N. W. (1929) 'The Birds of Port Stephens, N.S.W.' *Emu* 29: 243–251.

Christidis, L. & Boles, W. E. (1994) *The Taxonomy and Species of Birds of Australia and its Territories*. Royal Australasian Ornithologists Union Monograph 2. Hawthorn East, Victoria.

Christidis, L. & Boles, W. E. (2008) *Systematics and Taxonomy of Australian Birds*. CSIRO. Collingwood, Victoria.

Clarke, R. H. (2010) *The Status of Seabirds and Shorebirds at Ashmore Reef and Cartier and Browse Islands: Monitoring Program for the Montara Well release – Pre-impact Assessment and First Post-impact Field Survey*. Prepared on behalf of PTTEP Australasia and the Department of the Environment, Water, Heritage and the Arts, Australia.

Emison, W. B., et al. (1987) *Atlas of Victorian Birds*. Department of Conservation, Forests and Lands and the Royal Australasian Ornithologists Union. Melbourne.

Fullagar, P. J. 1976 'Seabird Islands No. 35, Cabbage Tree Island, New South Wales' *The Australian Bird Bander* 14: 94–7.

Garnett, S. T, Szabo, J. K. & Dutson, G. (2011) *The Action Plan for Australian Birds 2010*. CSIRO, Collingwood.

Higgins, P. J. (ed) (1999) *Handbook of Australian, New Zealand and Antarctic Birds Volume 4: Parrots to Dollarbird*. Oxford University Press. Melbourne.

Higgins, P. & Peter, J. M. (eds) (2002) *Handbook of Australian, New Zealand and Antarctic Birds Volume 6: Pardalotes to Shrike-thrushes*. Oxford University Press. Melbourne.

Hindwood, K. A. & Serventy, D. L. (1941) 'The Gould Petrel of Cabbage Tree Island'. *Emu* 41: 1–20.

Horadern, H. E. & Hordern, H. M. (1931) 'Birds of Port Stephens, N.S.W.' *Emu* 31: 21–6.

Hutton, I. (1991) *Birds of Lord How Island Past and Present*. Ian Hutton. Coffs

Harbour, NSW.

Johnstone, R. E. & Storr, G. M. (1998) *Handbook of Western Australian Birds. Volume I Non-Passerines (Emu to Dollarbird).* Western Australian Museum. Perth.

Johnstone, R. E. & Storr, G. M. (2004) *Handbook of Western Australian Birds. Volume II Passerines (Blue-winged Pitta to Goldfinch).* Western Australian Museum. Perth.

Marchant, S. & Higgins, P. J. (Coordinators) (1990) *Handbook of Australian, New Zealand and Antarctic Birds, Volume 1 Ratites to Ducks.* Oxford University Press. Melbourne.

Marchant, S. & Higgins, P. J. (1993) *Handbook of Australian, New Zealand and Antarctic Birds, Volume 2 Raptors to Lapwings.* Oxford University Press. Melbourne.

Onley, D. & Scofield, P. (2007) *Field Guide to the Albatrosses, Petrels and Shearwaters of the World.* Christopher Helm. London.

Pike, G. D. & Leach, G. J. (1997) *Handbook of the Vascular Plants of Ashmore and Cartier Islands.* Parks & Wildlife NT and Parks Australia.

Porter, J. G. (1983) *Discovering the Family Islands.* Kullari Publications. Tully.

Quinn, D. & Lacey, G. (1999) *Birds of French Island Wetlands.* Spectrum Publications. Richmond.

Simpson, K. & Day, N. (2010) *Field Guide to the Birds of Australia.* 8th ed. Viking. Camberwell.

Strahan, R. (ed) (1983) *The Australian Museum Complete Book of Australian Mammals.* The National Photographic Index of Australian Wildlife. Angus & Robertson Publishers. Sydney.

Taylor, S. (2013) *Best 100 Birdwatching Sites in Australia.* New South Publishing, Sydney.

Thomas, R., et al. (2011) *The Complete Guide to Finding the Birds of Australia.* CSIRO Publishing. Collingwood, Victoria.

Acknowledgements

Many people have assisted me with birding on Australia's islands. Without Steve Reynolds I would never have seen my first Chinese Pond Heron. Klaus Uhlenhut from Kirrama Tours is due credit for showing me my first Yellow Chat. Thanks go to Lloyd Nielsen for pointing out my first Collared Imperial Pigeon. Without Jenny Spry I'd never have identified Red-flanked Lorikeets on Saibai. I probably would not have seen the Rosy Starling or the Brown Shrike on Cocos without James Mustafa. And I will be forever grateful to New Zealander Dave Richards for ensuring that I added the Lesser Redpoll to my list on Macquarie Island.

Richard Baxter runs Birding Tours Australia. He is a superb birder. He took me to Christmas, Cocos, Boigu, Saibai and Raine Islands. He is responsible for showing me no fewer than 49 birds on my Australian list. That's not bad. (Note that this is not all the lifers I've seen on these five islands as I've been to Boigu and Christmas Islands with other guides as well. They got me the easy ones!)

Mike Carter has seen more Australian birds than anyone else, yet he always has time for the novice and greets my questions with great patience. So does Dr Rohan Clarke. He's always ready to answer questions I often feel a goose for having to ask.

Thanks are due to Ian Hutton, Mick Roderick and Tania Ireton for providing up-to-date information when I didn't know where else to turn. George Swann took me to Ashmore Reef twice, and Geoff Lacey did his best to show me a King Quail on French Island. It was Dr Rob Hamilton who pointed out that the birds on Macquarie Island that I thought were Common Redpolls were more likely to be Lesser Redpolls, sending me scurrying to the experts for confirmation. Both my brother, Richard Schurmann, and my friend Graham Barwell, were very helpful with technical advice when my computer skills were lacking.

And the photographers. I'm sure you'll agree that there are some superb photos in this book. Special thanks are due to Steve Reynolds and Brook Whylie, sine qua non. I'm also indebted to (in alphabetical order): Rohan Clarke, Ken Haines, Rob Hamilton, Judy Leitch, James Mustafa, Mick Roderick, Jack Shick, Paul Walbridge and Jack Winterbottom

But one person really stands out when I consider the 22 islands included in this book. Remember that I have not stepped foot on Browse, Raine or Cabbage Tree Islands. This man did not accompany me to Macquarie Island, Ashmore Reef, Chat Island or Saibai. Over several decades he escorted me to the other 15 islands, from Phillip Island in 1975 to the Abrolhos in 2008. He is my ever-suffering non-birding husband, Roger, to whom I owe boundless gratitude. Simple thanks is quite inadequate, yet I offer it here: thank you, Roger.

Index